THE KINGDOM, THE POWER AND THE GLORY

THE KINGDOM, THE POWER AND THE GLORY

By

Mel Bailey

Destiny Image Publishers
P.O. Box 351
Shippensburg, PA 17257

"Speaking to the Purposes of God for this Generation"

ISBN 1-56043-058-3

For Worldwide Distribution
Printed in the U.S.A.

CONTENTS

CONTENTS

FOREWORD

What are the keys that unlock the Lord's Prayer to become a lifestyle of revolutionary Christian living? Jesus instructed us to pray for the Kingdom to "come on earth as it is in heaven." But how does the Kingdom come? Where is the power in the Church? Why does the glory of God seem so illusive and intangible in daily Christian experience?

Mel Bailey gives us the keys to unlock the potential in Christian living in *The Kingdom, the Power and the Glory.* At a time of oppressive weariness and discouragement among many believers, God is giving the most exciting direction in the history of the Church to His bride. The witness of the Kingdom of God is our assignment at a critical time for all people around the world. As darkness covers the earth in political and economic tyranny, God is saying to His Church, "Arise, shine, for your light has come!"

Mel Bailey has devoted his life and ministry to seeking answers to the mysteries of the Kingdom of God to share in simplicity at such a time as this.

Several years ago a member of my congregation gave me tapes of sermons that this servant of the Lord had preached. With great trepidation of soul, I had been speaking many of the same Kingdom principles Mel Bailey shared boldly in those sermons. Confirmation — at a time when I needed it most — instantly translated into gratitude to God for the ministry and insights He had given to this minister so seasoned in God's Word. Those sermons became a tremendous source of strength to me as a gift from the Lord.

Since that time, Mel Bailey has become a trusted friend and co-laborer in the Lord's harvest. I have invited him to share often in conferences, seminars and services at Chapel Hill Harvester Church in Atlanta. His apostolic insights into God's Word, as well as his love and encouragement for young pastors and teachers, has established a firm foundation in numerous ministries for building a bold witness to Kingdom truth.

I believe that in the days to come, Mel Bailey will be regarded as a pioneer in the movement of Kingdom communication and demonstration in the body of Christ. If I am correct, *The Kingdom, the Power and the Glory* will become a classic manual in unlocking the mysteries of the Kingdom. And what will be the results of such teaching? The prayer that Jesus taught us to pray will become a reality of both God's power and His glory in ministry and in daily Christian living.

Our King Cometh!

Bishop Earl Paulk
Chapel Hill Harvester Church
Atlanta, Georgia

CHAPTER ONE

Seek First the Kingdom

Concerning the Kingdom

One of the most important truths for us to understand as believers is the message of the KINGDOM. Open the Bible almost anywhere and you will find references to the Kingdom of God. Jesus mentions the "kingdom of heaven" 28 different times in the four gospels and uses the expression "kingdom of God" 73 times. These two terms together are used over a hundred times in the gospels!

Jesus said, "Seek first His kingdom and His righteousness" (Matt. 6:33). Notice that Jesus says to "seek first" the Kingdom, so it obviously must be something of great importance for us. He taught His disciples to pray, in what we call "The Lord's Prayer," "Thy kingdom come, Thy will be done" (Matt. 6:10). How can we pray for the coming of His Kingdom unless we understand what it is? After His resurrection, Jesus presented Himself alive with many infallible proofs, "appearing to them over a period of forty days, and speaking of the things concerning the Kingdom of

God" (Acts 1:3). It seems that after the resurrection of Jesus, all He talked about was the Kingdom of God.

The subject of the Kingdom of God was important enough that Jesus said we should seek it first and pray for its coming; after His resurrection He spoke of it for forty days. The last words He said to His disciples before ascending to the Father concerned the Kingdom. If Jesus put so much emphasis on teaching His disciples about it, we should want to understand this important truth as well.

In Matthew chapter 13, Jesus gave illustration after illustration concerning His Kingdom. In verse 31 He said, "The kingdom of heaven is like a mustard seed." In verse 33 He said, "The kingdom of heaven is like leaven [yeast]." In verse 44 He said, "The Kingdom of heaven is like a treasure hidden in the field." In verse 45 Jesus said, "The kingdom of heaven is like a merchant seeking fine pearls." Finally, in verse 47 He said, "The kingdom of heaven is like a dragnet cast into the sea." Jesus gave six analogies in this thirteenth chapter of Matthew, ending with the parable of the dragnet. When He finished giving all these illustrations, in verse 51 Jesus asked His disciples, "Now, have you understood all these things?" And the disciples said, "Uh huh." They had about as much perception as many Christians in this generation. They did not hear a thing He said. They listened. They watched. But they did not hear what He was trying to tell them.

The disciples missed what Jesus was saying because they were focused on something else. Christians today miss the message of the Kingdom of God because they also have a faulty focus. They are focused on the future. Ask Christians today what the Kingdom of God is and the response will probably be "Heaven," and if the same subject came up in a room full of preachers, there would be as many concepts about it as the number of people present!

God is looking for people who are looking for the Kingdom! Simeon knew by revelation that he would not see death until he saw the Lord's Christ. He was in the temple when Joseph and Mary walked in with the baby Jesus to have Him circumcised when He was eight days old. Simeon knew that this was He for whom he had been looking. Another man with the same type of insight was Joseph of Arimathea. In the gospel of Luke we read, "Behold, a man named Joseph, who was a member of the Council, a good and righteous man (he had not consented to their plan and action), a man from Arimathea, a city of the Jews, who was waiting for the KINGDOM of God; THIS MAN went to Pilate and asked for the body of Jesus" (Luke 23:50-52). Isn't this an amazing passage of Scripture? The disciples had all fled! Judas had just betrayed Him! Peter had just denied Him! All of these men were the ones who were closest to Him and heard Him teach constantly concerning the KINGDOM. Yet EVERY SINGLE ONE OF THEM MISSED IT! But here is one man, Joseph of Arimathea, a man who was "waiting for the kingdom"; and it was HE who went to Pilate and said, "I WANT HIS BODY!" Joseph had great perception. He knew that the body hanging on that tree was directly tied to the Kingdom, which was what HE WAS WAITING FOR!

Jesus wanted the disciples to see the Kingdom in their midst. Think about this ... Jesus spent the 40 days after His resurrection talking about the Kingdom of God. He did not bother to say one word to them about the size of their mansions in glory. He was not holding a prayer seminar, nor was He conducting a church growth workshop. He spent the LAST FORTY DAYS on one vitally important subject. For forty consecutive days Jesus spent many hours speaking of the things concerning the Kingdom of God. Doesn't it sound as though He were putting some urgency on understanding this message?

Envision Jesus' last few moments on earth. He has disciples assembled around Him. He tells them to go to Jerusalem and tarry until they become endued with power from on high. He said, "But you shall receive power when the Holy Spirit has come upon you; and you shall be my witnesses..." (Acts 1:8). He also tells them what they are going to do when this Holy Spirit comes. Then a cloud comes down and Jesus steps onto it. As He starts to ascend, the disciples suddenly panic! They say, "Hey, wait a minute! What about the Kingdom? Where are You going? Will you restore the Kingdom UNTO ISRAEL?" They missed it again. All they could think about was getting Romans out of Jerusalem!

Too Heavenly-Minded

How utterly tragic! Jesus never was implying that His Kingdom was to be a Jewish one. Surely they should have known the prophecy of Daniel that "to Him was given dominion, Glory and a kingdom, that ALL the peoples, NATIONS (plural) and men of EVERY language might serve Him" (Dan. 7:14). No wonder Jesus replied to the disciples, "It is not for you to know times or epochs which the Father has fixed by His own authority" (Acts 1:7). They were not comprehending Kingdom theology.

Many Christians today can think only of getting themselves off this earth. All they want is to get to heaven. They think that the Kingdom of God is heaven. But even at face value, that makes very little sense.

Why would Jesus spend all His time telling His disciples about what happens after they die? Is our whole purpose on earth simply to wait our turn to go to heaven? Obviously not. But today's Church has been like those first disciples who were standing looking up at the sky when Jesus ascended. We have been standing around waiting for something to happen. God is waiting for US to happen! He spoke to the children of Israel and reaffirmed to the Church that He is after a Kingdom of priests and a holy nation (Ex. 19:6, 1 Pet. 2:9). Those do not come about by dying, but by living for Him! This is why Paul said that "the kingdom of God is not eating and drinking, but righteousness and peace and joy in the Holy Spirit" (Rom. 14:17). That is the simplest definition of the Kingdom of God... It is a lifestyle! It begins right now.

Let's examine how this happens. The moment we were saved, we were instantly translated from the kingdom of darkness into the Kingdom of His dear Son (Col. 1:13). It is an instantaneous conversion that translates us from the realm of darkness into the realm of light, which is the Kingdom of God. The term, "the Kingdom of GOD" denotes ownership. It is GOD'S KINGDOM — nobody else's. The expression, "kingdom of heaven" simply denotes the source of the Kingdom — where it comes from. When we pray the Lord's Prayer, "Thy kingdom come. Thy will be done, on earth as it is heaven," we are praying for the same kind of lifestyle here that exists in heaven.

The Meek Shall Inherit the Earth

How is that possible? Go back to the very beginning. When God placed Adam and Eve in the garden, it was His intention to give them dominion authority over the entire earth and over everything pertaining to it.

When Adam and Eve disobeyed God, they gave that dominion and authority over to the devil. Although we know that Satan is the "god of this world," we should not confuse that with the issue of who owns this planet! The earth BELONGS to the Lord, and the earth is the INHERITANCE of the saints. Jesus said the meek shall inherit the earth (Matt. 5:5). When we say that Satan is the god of this world, we mean that he has power only over the wicked. Satan is the god of unregenerate man's system, but he does not own this planet.

God has already given us all things that pertain to life and godliness! When we speak of the Kingdom of God being "now," we must go back and see what Jesus purchased for us. He came that we might have life, and have it more abundantly. That does NOT mean we are going to have life some day or in the sweet by-and-by. We have life *now* through the Person of Jesus Christ.

We limit God when we focus all our attention on the future. Psalm 145:13 says, "Thy kingdom is an everlasting kingdom, and Thy dominion endures throughout all generations." When we think in terms of the Kingdom of God, we must remember that God is, God has always been, and God always will be. Jesus taught that "the kingdom of God is within us" (Luke 17:21). When the early Church began to minister the Word, their proclamation was "Repent, for the kingdom of heaven is at hand."

We're dealing with two aspects of the Kingdom of God here. The moment we are saved we are born into the Kingdom of God, translated from the kingdom of darkness into the Kingdom of His dear Son. Instantly we are a part of the Kingdom of God. However, the greatest event is just ahead of us. There comes a time in the future when the saints will literally possess the Kingdom (Dan. 7:18).

This is a vital truth to which we must lay hold! Most of us have friends or relatives who at one time gave their hearts to the Lord but, because they had no sustained revelation of the Kingdom of God, they have gone right back to the hog pen where they were before they ever gave their heart to the Lord. Matthew 13:19 says, "When anyone hears the word of the kingdom, and does not understand it, the evil one comes and snatches away what has been sown in his heart..." The message of the Kingdom is probably the most misunderstood message of any truth in the Word of God.

Proper Motivation

Satan seeks to bluff believers out of the Kingdom, getting them to settle for a "blessing level" of Christianity. This is the baby Christian level of "bless me, bless me, bless me". It must be much more than that. We are called to take possession of the Kingdom! When our understanding is wrong, our motivation is wrong. It is like the fellow who told his son to go clean out the garage. He said, "I want that garage cleaned out by four o'clock Monday afternoon." Well, the kid saw all the junk that needed to be cleaned out and said to himself, "Why do I have to do this? I didn't make this mess." All weekend he put it off. Monday arrived and his father looked at the garage. Then he told his son that if it does not get cleaned out, he will not be able to put in the new car! It was amazing how fast that boy could work!

We need to realize that, even though the new car has not arrived, it is ours now! We need to get ready. We need to take possession. Not everyone agrees with this approach, however. Some think that all we are called to do is wait. The critics of the Kingdom Now message say, "You can't have a Kingdom until the King comes." Yet John the Baptist declared, "Repent, for the kingdom of heaven is at hand" (Matt. 3:2). When Jesus began His ministry He also preached, "Repent, for the kingdom of heaven is at hand" (Matt. 4:17). In Matthew 10:7 Jesus instructed the twelve disciples: "And as you go, preach, saying, 'The kingdom of heaven is at hand.' " Later, when Jesus sent the seventy out two by two, He instructed them in Luke 10:9: "...and heal those in it [the city] who are sick, and say to them, 'The kingdom of God has come near to you.' " How can the Kingdom be "AT HAND" if it is thousands of years away? Does not the expression "AT HAND" mean "at the present time"? God has wanted us to see that the Kingdom is in our present time.

The Progression of Revelation

This has not been a popular message, but then truth has always been accepted grudgingly by the Church. Every time God does something fresh, traditionalists fight it. The early Church walked with great anointing and had tremendous revelation, but by the fourth century it was almost completely lost. There was almost a total eclipse of truth during the Dark Ages. The first restored truth, salvation by faith, was proclaimed in 1517 by Martin Luther. One hundred years later the next major truth to be restored was that of water baptism. It was in the 1700s that John and Charles Wesley opened up the revelation of holiness, or sanctification. Then revelation began to be added more quickly. In the 1800s the doctrine of the second coming of Christ began to be written about, as well as that of divine healing. Each one of these truths was met by resistance from the religious establishment! The group that received one facet of truth would not accept the next flow of revelation because it did not originate in their camp!

The Lord has continued to reveal His truth in this century. John Alexander Dowie was the preacher who initiated the healing ministry at the end of the 1800s. A plague had swept through his church in Australia and over forty people died. At one of the funerals a sixteen-year-old girl had gone into convulsions and had to be taken home. By the time Dowie arrived, the doctor was standing there shaking his head, saying, "God's will be done." Dowie said, "God doesn't have anything to do with this. This is the work of the devil." He jumped over on that bed and he took authority over the spirit of death. The girl immediately snapped out of her convulsions. From that incident a mighty healing ministry was launched. He came to the United States in 1898 and held his first crusade in San Francisco. Then he went to Chicago (about 1900) and put up a large tent across from the World's Fair. Thousands were healed there. Out of this ministry came men like F.F. Bosworth, John G. Lake, Gordon Lindsay and many other pioneers of the healing ministry.

In 1906, the outpouring of the Holy Spirit came at Azusa Street in Los Angeles, California. This was the birth of the modern Pentecostal Movement. But there were a lot of confused people in the Church world. Many of the established denominations said, "This is of the devil!" Yet by the 1960s this outpouring of the Holy Spirit had penetrated every denomination. This generation has seen God speak something fresh every ten years. The Latter Rain Movement began in 1948. This movement initiated the identifying of the gifts and ministries by apostles and prophets that God began to raise up at that time. Callings were identified in people's lives and gifts were bestowed by impartation. Remember Paul instructed Timothy to stir up the gift that came by the laying on of hands. There was an impartation. It is the Holy Spirit who gives the gifts, but many times they come through human instrumentality by the laying on of hands. There was a lot of reaction to this movement. Ironically, the first people to reject it were the last people who had had a fresh revelation.

In the 1950s God began to restore praise and worship. Many Charismatics have just come into the restoration of praise and worship in the last few years, which is beautiful, but there were churches that had begun this type of worship in the early 1950s. Then in the 1960s came another wave of revelation called the deliverance ministry. Praying for healing over and over again for someone oppressed by demon power is futile. There will be no healing until the demon is dealt with and cast out.

Notice the pattern here. When praise and worship came, the traditionalists rejected it. They said, "That's not God; what's that crazy sound?" They did not like to hear people singing in the Spirit. Unfortunately, some of the same people who were moving in praise and worship criticized the deliverance ministry when it arrived. They said, "Oh boy, they're looking for demons behind every bush." (There were a few demons behind a few bushes, by the way.)

The Present Day Church

In the 1970s came two other truths. God began to speak the faith message, and the Discipleship Movement came on the scene. Yes, there were some excesses in these teachings. Every time a fresh revelation comes, there seems to be a heavy pendulum swing that takes time to return to center. In the discipleship teaching there was oppression when people were lorded over by ministries. There were church people who became so "ministry oriented" that they lost the ability to hear from God. In the name of "submitting to authority," they finally wound up going to spiritual authority (pastor, elder, etc.) and asking questions almost as ridiculous as, "What color shall I paint my kitchen cupboards?" Obviously, the imbalance was caused by people allowing prophetic words that ministries gave them to rule their lives, rather than spending time on their faces before God and allowing Him to talk to them and using the prophetic words to confirm what God had already spoken.

Those who embraced the revelations of the 1970s came under heavy attack, just as we have now as God began speaking in the 1980s and 1990s about unity in the body of Christ and the gospel of the Kingdom. Traditionalists are resisting these words today, but we should not be surprised. Just as God confirmed the work of the Holy Spirit that was begun in 1906, He will confirm what He is speaking now about His Body and the Kingdom of God.

Notice that fresh insight and revelation has been coming rapidly in the last handful of years. Every truth that has come down through history has been revealed to prepare THIS generation to possess the land! Why should we be reading books and attending seminars to find out who we are in Christ if we are going to disappear at any minute? Does it make sense to blow a trumpet in Zion and sound the alarm on His holy mountain so we can desert? In the army they shoot deserters! God is trying to raise up an army, one that does not want to "fly away" but finally to "occupy." The Kingdom Now message is not new, but a restored truth from the very beginning. It is the "by-and-by" concept that is relatively new, which is what we will examine next.

CHAPTER TWO

What About the Rapture?

Songbook Theology

Whether we admit it or not, much of our theology about the end times does not come from the Bible, but from the songbook. We have songbook theology, not Scripture theology! The pathetic picture of the sweet by-and-by has come from unscriptural songs. We need to get rid of these false ideas before we can truthfully examine what the Scriptures have to say.

These songs originated prior to the Civil War. Black people were literally sold like cattle in the southern states of America. Husbands and wives were separated, and children were taken from the arms of their parents — all at the owner's whim. These precious black brothers and sisters did not know whether they would ever see their families again when they were sold and their families broken up. They had a simple faith in God and in their hope of heaven. They knew that to be absent from the body was to be present with the Lord. Born out of that oppression and despair came many of the songs known as the Negro Spirituals; for example, "Swing low, sweet chariot, coming for to carry me home. A band of angels comin' after me." They have catchy melodies, but these songs had actually dual meanings. For example, "Steal away, steal away, steal away to Jesus" meant two things. If they could escape their bondage and steal away to the North, perhaps they would find some of their family there. If they were caught and hung, it was "steal away home, I ain't got long to stay here."

Those songs were borne of extreme despair. "Nobody knows the trouble I've seen..." The only way they could get their families together would be to die and find each other. The songs were written because of the hopelessness of the black families' condition during those times. Then songs with that same mentality began to be incorporated into the mainstream of Protestantism. Pick up any hymnal and notice the number of titles that have to do with the idea of "going home." I started counting and got to 140 before I decided to quit!

Another example is, "Somewhere the sun is shining, somewhere the sky is blue." The chorus goes, "Somewhere, somewhere, beautiful isle of some-where." Where is any glimpse of His glorious Kingdom? How about, "I'll Fly Away" and "In the Sweet By-and-by?" There will be one generation that will NOT die! There will be a generation that will be the welcoming committee when Jesus returns to establish His Kingdom. Why do people get so excited over songs that talk about dying? We should get excited over the hymns like "He Lives." Because He lives, so shall we live — forever!

What about heaven? Yes, it exists and we believe in it. Heaven is real, but it is for the spirits of the righteous. The Lord is going to bring all of those who

have died with Him when He comes! There is a
Kingdom that the Lord wants here on the earth. He
wants a Kingdom of priests and a holy nation. Our
picture of heaven is not from the Scriptures, it's from
the songbook. "I've a home prepared where the saints
abide, just over in the glory land." "Glory land" is
another word for a songbook favorite, "Beulah land."
"Beulah" is actually used only once in the Bible, and
the word means "married." Somewhere in Church
music composition, someone wrote a song about it and
made a place out of what was meant to be a condition.

God wants to be married to His people; that is the
meaning of "Beulah." But instead of this beautiful
image of the bride of Christ, we have a picture of a
place in the by-and-by. "O Beulah land, sweet Beulah
land, as on the highest mount I stand. I look away
across the sea where mansions are prepared for me."
The song may sound nice and have a pleasant melody,
yet the reality is that there is no such place as Beulah
land! There is no more of a Beulah land than there is a
Radio land. Glory land, Beulah land, and Radio land
are all right next to each other.

God's Plan for the Planet

Let's get rid of our songbook theology so we can
understand what God's Word is saying. God has a
purpose for the planet Earth. Some think that it is just
going to burn up. No, it won't! Ecclesiastes 1:4 says,
"...The earth remains forever." But people ask, "Doesn't
the Bible say that the earth is going to be destroyed
with fire?" Peter talks about the elements of the earth
melting with intense heat in Second Peter 3:10. But
right before that, in verses five and six, Peter states,
"the earth was formed out of water and by water,
through which the world at that time was destroyed,

being flooded with water. But the present heavens and earth by His word are being reserved for fire..." Note that he says that the world was destroyed by the flood. Did the earth disappear after the flood? Of course not; all God did was clean house with the flood.

It is like a city that is made up completely of old buildings that no longer measure up to any kind of safety code. The bulldozers would come in and level the whole city and then build a new one. This is what God has done and is going to do! The world of the ungodly was destroyed by the flood. All that happened to the earth was that the people who messed it up were removed from it. The final judgment of the ungodly will be exactly the same way. When the Lord judges the earth by fire, it will be to deal with the wicked so that He might establish His Kingdom, of which the Word speaks. Jesus said, "...Blessed are the gentle (or meek), for they shall inherit the earth" (Matt. 5:5). He did not say they would inherit heaven, He said "the EARTH."

We are talking about a literal Kingdom of God that is being prepared to rule over the earth. We are the meek that Jesus spoke about. We are that chosen generation. We are the people of God, and God is getting ready to rid the earth of every contamination. God will remove those who do not want to walk with Him. They will be cut off. God has a special place for those who do not want to have anything to do with Him. It is not planet earth! They are leaving, we are staying. The meek SHALL inherit the earth!

Who's Leaving and Who's Staying

The twenty-fourth chapter of Matthew tells us about these two groups of people. Jesus begins by spelling out a time of great trouble such as there has never been in the history of the world. Then, beginning in verse 37, Jesus states, "For the coming of the Son of Man will be just like the days of Noah." What were the "days of Noah" like? They were "eating and drinking, they were marrying and giving in marriage," they were doing their own thing. They had their beach houses, their summer houses, their yachts, etc. Jesus explained what would happen: "And they did not understand until the flood came and took them all away; so shall the coming of the Son of Man be. Then there shall be two men in the field; one will be taken, and one will be left" (vv. 39-40). We have traditionally been taught that this is where the rapture takes place. The next verse says, "Two women will be grinding at the mill; one will be taken, and one will be left." Again, this has been explained as the time that the rapture takes place. The believers are supposedly taken up to be with the Lord and the unbelievers are left behind here on the earth.

But that does not make sense. Reexamine the illustration Jesus gave us. He said, "For the coming of the Son of Man will be just like the days of Noah." When we look at the conditions that existed during Noah's day, we begin to realize that when judgment came, the people who left were the wicked. The people who stayed on the earth were the righteous. If the righteous were not the ones left, none of us would be here now. Drowned people cannot bear children. Noah, his wife, and their sons Ham, Shem, and Japheth and their wives — eight souls in all — got on the ark. They were the ones that were left.

If we examined the Scriptures without our song-books, we would find that the Word of God is totally consistent concerning who is leaving and who is staying. For years the Church has been singing, "I'll

Fly Away." But according to the Word, it is not we who are doing the flying! Job 20:4-7 says, "Do you know this from of old, from the establishment of man on earth, that the triumphing of the wicked is short, and the joy of the godless momentary? Though his loftiness reaches the heavens, and his head touches the clouds, he perishes forever like his refuse; those who have seen him will say, 'Where is he?' " Verse 8 says, "He flies away like a dream." The next time you hear, "I'll Fly Away," remember, that the wicked are the ones who are leaving!

Let us go back for a moment to that passage in Matthew 24. "Then there shall be two men in the field; one will be TAKEN, and one will be left. Two women will be grinding at the mill; one will be TAKEN, and one will be left." We are used to interpreting that passage to mean that the righteous one is the one taken, but it is the *unrighteous* one who is taken away. We have transposed the meaning of the verse. For example, the following sentence may be interpreted two different ways, "Johnny said the teacher is a fool," depending on the punctuation. (1) "Johnny", said the teacher, "is a fool." or (2) Johnny said, "The teacher is a fool." In the first sentence, the teacher is accusing Johnny of being a fool. In the second sentence, Johnny returns the favor and accuses the teacher of being a fool. So, who is "taken"? The wicked! Who is left? The righteous!

All Scripture is consistent with itself. When referring to the wicked, the various passages do not contradict each other. In Matthew 24:37-41, it is very obvious that it is the wicked who are taken away or removed. Also in Proverbs 10:30, it is clearly stated that the righteous will never be removed. Jesus, in Matthew 13:47-49, is giving us still another picture of this same principle of the wicked being removed. Let us take a close look at what He said. "Again, the kingdom of heaven is like a dragnet cast into the sea, and gathering fish of every kind; and when it was filled, they drew it up on the beach; and they sat down, and gathered the good fish into containers, but the bad they threw away." Now, let's just review what Jesus said! Which fish did they keep? The GOOD fish! Which fish did they throw away? The BAD fish. Verse 49 states, "So it will be at the end of the age; the angels shall come forth, and take out the wicked from among the righteous." So, who's leaving? THE WICKED! Who's staying? THE RIGHTEOUS! Who is going to inherit the earth? The righteous! Psalm 10:16 gives even further clarity, for it reads, "The Lord IS King forever and ever; nations have perished from HIS land." Why were they removed? Because those nations who rose up against God were simply removed from HIS property. Numbers 14:21 declares, "But indeed, as I live, all the earth will be filled with the glory of the Lord."

Once again, all Scripture is totally consistent with itself. A careful study of the 37th Psalm graphically brings us to this conclusion. Let's begin with Psalm 37:8-10: "Cease from anger, and forsake wrath; do not fret, it leads only to evildoing. For *evildoers* will be cut off, but those who wait for the Lord, *they* will inherit the land. Yet a little while and the *wicked* man will be no more; and you will look carefully for his place, and he will not be there." If we are leaving any minute, how can we look for the *wicked* man's place if *we* have been taken away? Verses 11-40 continue: "But the *humble* will inherit the land, and will delight themselves in abundant prosperity. The *wicked* plots against the *righteous*, and gnashes at him with his teeth. The Lord laughs at him; for He sees *his* day is coming. The *wicked* have drawn the sword and bent their bow, to cast down the afflicted and the needy, to slay those who are upright in conduct. *Their* sword will enter their *own* heart, and their bows will be broken. Better is the little of the righteous than the abundance of many wicked. For the arms of the *wicked* will be broken; but the Lord sustains the *righteous*. The Lord knows the days of the *blameless*; and *their* inheritance will be forever. They will not be ashamed in the time of evil; and in the days of famine they will have abundance. But the *wicked* will perish; and the enemies of the Lord will be like the glory of the pastures, *they* vanish — like smoke they vanish away. The wicked borrows and does not pay back, but the righteous is gracious and gives. For those blessed by Him will inherit the land; but those cursed by Him will be cut off. The steps of a man are established by the Lord; and he delights in his way. When he falls, he shall not be hurled headlong; because the Lord is the One who holds his hand. I have been young, and now I am old; yet I have not seen the *righteous* forsaken, or his descendants begging bread. All day long he is gracious and lends; and his descendants are a blessing. Depart from evil, and do good, so *you* will abide forever. For the Lord loves justice, and does not forsake His godly ones; they are preserved *forever*; but the descendants of the *wicked* will be *cut off*. The *righteous* will inherit the land, and *dwell in it forever*. The mouth of the righteous utters wisdom, and his tongue speaks justice. The law of his God is in his heart; his steps do not slip. The wicked spies upon the righteous, and seeks to kill him. The Lord will not leave him in his hand, or let him be condemned when he is judged. Wait for the Lord, and keep His way, and He will exalt *you* to inherit the land; When the *wicked* are *cut off*, *you will see it*. I have seen a violent, *wicked* man spreading himself like a luxuriant tree in its native soil. Then he passed away, and lo, *he was no more*; I sought for him, but *he could not be found*. Mark the *blameless* man, and behold the upright; for the man of *peace will have a posterity*. But *transgressors* will be altogether *destroyed*; the posterity of the *wicked* will be *cut off*. But the salvation of the *righteous* is from the Lord; He is their strength in time of trouble. And the Lord helps them, and delivers them; He delivers them *from* the wicked, and saves them, because they take refuge in Him."

Nine times in this 37th Psalm, it says that the RIGHTEOUS inherit the land FOREVER! There are twelve pronounced judgments upon the wicked; there are eighteen pronounced blessings upon the righteous. All of these Scriptures are consistent with the principle of God's judgments upon the wicked...THEY will be removed from His property, because the earth IS the Lord's, and He has promised it as an inheritance to the righteous. James 2:5 says, "Listen, my beloved brethren: did not God choose the poor of this world to be rich in faith and heirs of the kingdom which He promised to those who love Him?" Proverbs 2:22 says, "But the wicked will be cut off from the land, and the treacherous will be uprooted from it." We have been so caught up (no pun intended) in recent years in the idea of getting "snatched" that we do not see the picture the Bible paints. Let us suppose that someone comes to a house about midnight and knocks at the door. A man who has been asleep for an hour or so comes to the door. When he opens the door he finds a man dressed in blue wearing a badge on his cap, a gun strapped to his waist, and a big billy club hanging down to his knees. He takes out some chrome bracelets and puts them on the man at the door and TAKES him away. Now you know he is *not* being raptured!

This is the destiny that awaits the wicked. God explains in Isaiah 24:4-6 that He plans to judge the wicked of the earth for having defiled planet earth. "The earth mourns and withers, the world fades and withers, the exalted of the people of the earth fade away. The earth is also polluted by its inhabitants, for they transgressed laws, violated statutes, broke the everlasting covenant. Therefore, a curse devours the earth, and those who live in it are held guilty. Therefore, the inhabitants of the earth are burned, *and few men are left.*" The ones *left* will be the *righteous.* The ecology movement did not begin on Earth Day, as the media would have us believe. God has had an ecology program from the beginning. He is going to hold the people responsible on the earth who have contaminated it. God removed the wicked by water last time. This time around He is going to remove them by fire. But someone is left. "The meek...shall inherit the earth." The only people who will live on planet earth will be righteous people. The wicked will simply be removed.

Most people have difficulty with this message because they are so filled with songbook theology. Remember that old song, "This old world can never hold me, any moment I'll be gone?" Once we get a revelation of what the Word is saying, we ought to strip bumper stickers off cars that say, "In the event of the rapture, this car will not be manned," and stick another one on there that says, "Yes, it will!" We inherit the earth — the wicked are the ones who have to leave.

What was the promise given when Jesus physically left this planet? When the disciples were watching Jesus ascend out of their presence in Acts chapter One, the two men in white clothing stood beside them saying, "Men of Galilee, why do you stand looking into the sky? This Jesus, who has been taken up from you into heaven, will come in just the same way as you have watched Him go into heaven." Revelation 1:7 says, "Behold, He is coming with the clouds, and every eye will see Him..." The most dramatic days are just around the corner. And with the five billion people now on the earth and the restlessness that is upon all nations, we are getting close to His glorious return! Judgment is coming, but it is for the ungodly. For God's people there is immunity.

Do Not Be Ignorant

Paul prefaced his statement about what was going to happen at Christ's return with the words, "But we do not want you to be uninformed [KJV — "ignorant"], brethren." (1 Thess. 4:13) It is incredible that, despite those words, the Church has been incredibly ignorant in interpreting the following four verses. It is as though the Lord is pleading, "Please don't be ignorant about this!" Paul goes on to say, "We do not want you to be uninformed [or ignorant], brethren, about those who are asleep, that you may not grieve, as do the rest who have no hope. For if we believe that Jesus died and rose again, even so GOD WILL BRING WITH HIM THOSE WHO HAVE FALLEN ASLEEP IN JESUS" (1 Thess. 4:13-14). Notice it says, "God will BRING with Him those who have fallen asleep in Jesus." This is a passage of Scripture that the Church has traditionally taught as pertaining to the rapture taking place.

But wait a minute. If this passage is describing the Lord's coming to get us and take us somewhere, why is He bringing everybody with Him from heaven? All through the Bible we read of the "second coming of Christ." Yet it has not been described as a coming, but rather a leaving. Most Christians read the passages above as revealing the time that we are cutting out of here! BUT THAT IS NOT WHAT THE WORD SAYS AT ALL. Verse 15 of First Thessalonians chapter Four says, "For this we say to you by the word of the Lord, that we who are ALIVE, and REMAIN until... (the "disappearing act of the Church?" Is that what it says? No, not at all!)... "until the coming of the Lord..."

The next verse describes His coming. "For the Lord Himself shall descend..." What direction? "Descend" means "come down." "The Lord Himself will descend from heaven..." If we wanted to sneak the Church out through the back end of town, secretly and quietly (as so many Bible teachers over the years have been telling us it is going to happen), then the Lord certainly is making a big mistake! Watch how the next two verses describe His coming. "For the Lord Himself will descend from heaven with a shout [that does not sound very secretive], with the voice of the archangel, and with the trumpet of God; and the dead in Christ shall rise first. Then we who are alive and remain shall be caught up..."

"Caught up." These last two words in that verse is where the whole rapture theology comes from. Preachers have built wild fantasies around these two words, "caught up." But let's look at what they really mean. "Then we who are alive and remain shall be caught up...in the clouds to meet the Lord in the air, and thus shall we always be with the Lord." Let us not go off into vain speculation. Most Christians have been taught that we are going to go to heaven and eat for seven years. They have been taught that when the rapture takes place the Lord is going to come and get the Church and take it to heaven, and the Jews are going to be left down here to go through the terrible tribulation. The same people who have taught that the Church is going to be raptured and taken up also tell us that the Holy Spirit is going to be withdrawn from the earth. Then the Jews are supposed to evangelize the rest of the world!

This is amazing! We have a world where the Church has left, the Holy Spirit is gone and a nation of Jews who have not opened their hearts to Christ yet themselves — then suddenly the Jews are just going to fall into place and evangelize the world. And they are going to do this with no Holy Spirit and no revelation of Christ! Let's hold this thought for a moment and go back to where we left off in First Thessalonians chapter Four. "We who are alive and remain shall be caught up together with them in the clouds to meet the Lord in the air, and thus we shall always be with the Lord." Most of us have been taught that we are going "up there" and we will eat for seven years while the tribulation is taking place. But if we examine the Scriptures, we will note carefully that none of this is anywhere in the Word!

The Real Rapture

Let's look at what it really does say in First Thessalonians 4:17. "Then we who are alive and remain shall be caught up together with them in the clouds to meet the Lord in the air, and thus we shall always be with the Lord." In verse 14 we read that He is bringing all of the dead in Christ with Him. Why? Very simply, He is getting ready to set up a kingdom! And we which are ALIVE and REMAIN are the welcoming committee! Our bodies are changed instantly, the minute we rise to meet Him. At that glorious time when the

Lord returns, we are going to be changed into His likeness instantly! The Bible says, "It has not appeared as yet what we shall be. We know that, when He appears, we shall be like Him..." (1 John 3:2) When? When He appears. "We who are alive and remain shall be caught up together with them in the clouds to meet the Lord in the air..." (1 Thess. 4:17). What will it be like? First Corinthians 15:51-53 says, "Behold, I tell you a mystery; we shall not all sleep [or die], but we shall all be changed, in a moment, in the twinkling of an eye, at the last trumpet; for the trumpet will sound, and the dead will be raised imperishable, and we shall be changed. For this perishable must put on the imperishable, and this mortal must put on immortality." This corruptible body will take on an incorruptible state — that quickly, in a moment, in a twinkling of an eye.

But let us get out of our heads the idea that Jesus is coming to catch the Church away. We need to re-examine the Scriptures that have been used to present this doctrine. Scriptures such as Ephesians 5:27 have been misquoted as saying that the Lord is coming FOR a Church. But read it again. It says, "that He might *present to* Himself the Church." There is not ONE SCRIPTURE that says the Lord is coming FOR a Church. We need to start writing more new songs. We need to base them on God's Word. When the Lord returns, the dead in Christ will rise first. We which are alive and yet remain shall be caught up together to welcome Him in that meeting in the air. He will judge the wicked simultaneously. As we are rising to meet the Lord, He is judging the earth in righteousness. This was His plan from the very beginning, which is where we need to look next...THE BEGINNING!

CHAPTER THREE

A Kingdom of Priests

Beginning at the Beginning

How important is it for us to understand the Kingdom of God? Consider what we know about Paul's last years of teaching. In the Book of Acts we read, "And when they had set a day for him [Paul], they came to him at his lodging in large numbers; and he was explaining to them by solemnly testifying about the kingdom of God, and trying to persuade them concerning Jesus, from both the Law of Moses and from the Prophets, from morning until evening" (Acts 28:23). Paul is teaching on two subjects: The Kingdom of God and Jesus. The leading men of the Jews in Rome desired to hear Paul's views concerning "this sect" (verse 22). They came to the house where he was living to hear and learn about the Kingdom of God. They were so hungry that he kept teaching and teaching, morning to evening! Verse 30 of Acts 28 says, "And he stayed two full years in his own rented quarters, and was welcoming all who came to him." For two full years he was preaching and teaching about the Kingdom of God. TWO FULL YEARS! What was Paul's source material for all this teaching? "...from both the Law of Moses and from the Prophets." This is where we need to begin.

In order to understand God's purpose for this planet, we need to go to the Book of Genesis. *Genesis* means "beginnings," and it is here that we can begin to see what God is speaking about on this subject of the Kingdom of God. Starting in verse 26 of Genesis chapter one we read, "Then God said, 'Let Us make man in Our image, according to Our likeness; and let them rule over the fish of the sea and over the birds of the sky and over the cattle and over all the earth, and over every creeping thing that creeps on the earth.' And God created man in His own image, in the image of God He created him; male and female He created them. And God blessed them; and God said to them, 'Be fruitful and multiply, and fill the earth, and subdue it; and rule over the fish of the sea and over the birds of the sky, and rule over every living thing that moves on the earth.' " It is obvious that when God created man and placed him on the earth, He gave him dominion authority over literally everything that moves. It is in these three verses (26-28) of Genesis chapter one, that we find the very root of the terminology of what is called "dominion theology." Note that it is not new — it is as old as the Book of Genesis!

In chapter three of Genesis we read of the fall of man. Adam and Eve were beguiled by the serpent and they subsequently relinquished their authority. They gave everything over to the devil. The curse resulted from their actions. The curse came on the ground. Weeds began to grow. The animals turned wild. The very first human being who was ever born, Cain, ended up a murderer. Something perverse had entered into the human heart. Therefore, the Scripture says, "We are born in sin and shapen in iniquity." "All have sinned and come short of the glory of God." Sin is, simply, missing the mark.

When God placed Adam and Eve on this planet, He gave them dominion authority over the whole earth. But they blew it. They handed dominion over to the devil. God's purpose is to restore what was lost to our first parents. Jesus said in Luke 19:10 that He came to "seek and to save THAT which was lost." We are not a THAT, we are people. Jesus died for our sins, but we have not understood the whole redemption plan. Romans chapter eight tells us that all creation is groaning and travailing, waiting for the manifestation of the sons of God. The earth is waiting for us! When Adam and Eve sold out to the devil, the curse did not only fall on man, but on the earth as well. We sing songs from Scripture about how the trees of the field will clap their hands. That is a prophecy about what is going to happen when the curse is broken from planet earth. We have never seen a free tree.

Inheriting the Earth

We have been brainwashed to abandon our inheritance. The meek shall INHERIT the earth. If a banker called us and told us that a rich uncle had left us with 20,000 acres in Texas, would we want to claim it? Of course — why not? God tells us that He wants us to have the whole world. In Genesis 13:14-15, God speaks to Abram, "Now lift up your eyes and look from the place where you are, northward and southward and eastward and westward; for all the land which you see, I will give it to you and to your descendants forever." That is quite a promise. God told Abram that He would give him ALL the land FOREVER. And it was not only for Abram himself, but for his descendants or seed.

The basis for "kingdom theology" as it is now being taught goes right back to the promise God gave to Abram, Isaac and Jacob in the book of beginnings, the Book of Genesis. After God made His will known to Abram concerning this planet in Genesis 13:14-17, He appeared to Isaac in Genesis 26:2. "And the Lord appeared to him and said, 'Do not go down to Egypt; stay in the land of which I shall tell you. Sojourn in this land and I will be with you and bless you, for to you and to your descendants I will give all these lands, and I will establish the oath which I swore to your father Abraham. And I will multiply your descendants as the stars of heaven, and will give your descendants all these lands; and by your descendants all the nations of the earth shall be blessed.''

The promise continues as we examine Genesis 28:12, where God reaffirms His promise to Abraham's grandson, Jacob. This text reads, "And he [Jacob] had a dream, and behold, a ladder was set on the earth with its top reaching to heaven; and behold, the angels of God were ascending and descending on it. And behold, the Lord stood above it and said, 'I am the Lord, the God of your father Abraham and the God of Isaac; the land on which you lie, I will GIVE it to you and to your descendants.'' The Lord is saying, in effect, "Hey Abram, listen up Isaac, and you too, Jacob (yeah, you with your head on a rock for a pillow) ...I'm going to GIVE all this REAL ESTATE TO YOUR DESCENDANTS FOREVER!''

Who are the descendants of Abraham? Galatians 3:29 says: "If you belong to Christ, then you are Abraham's offspring, heirs according to the promise.'' So if we belong to Jesus Christ, we are descendants of

Abraham, which qualifies us for his inheritance. In verse 17 of Genesis 13, God told Abram, "Arise, walk about the land through its length and breadth; for I will give it to you." The next five words of verse 18 say, "Then Abram moved his tent..." He not only took his measuring rod, but he took his tent stakes with him as he is measuring it out. He took immediate action on the word God gave him. So we see that from the very beginning of the Bible, God's plan was for the meek to inherit the whole earth.

The Kingdom Promise to Moses

The first use of the word "Kingdom" was addressed to Moses. The children of Israel had become a great number of people. In Exodus 19:5-6 God tells these people about His plans and purposes — the Kingdom message. Moses was instructed to tell the people, "Now then, if you will indeed obey My voice and keep My covenant, then you shall be My own possession among all the peoples, for **all the earth is Mine;**" This is critical — "All the earth is Mine." God then goes on, "and you shall be to Me a kingdom of priests..." Most of us know from our Bible study that the Levites were the tribe designated to be priests, but that was not God's original intention. Moses was told to tell the people that God desired all twelve tribes to be priests. He wanted a KINGDOM of priests, not just one tribe. That was the Lord's second plan. His first plan was for *all* His people to be priests.

But when the people saw on Mount Sinai what God had in mind, they bowed out. They told Moses, in effect, "No, we can't handle that. You go talk to God. We don't want to do that lest we die" (see Exodus 20:19). So as second choice, the Levites were called in. Isn't this tragic? God wanted to establish a kingdom

under the authority of man when He put Adam and
Eve in the garden. They failed. Now He has a nation
with which He is going to try to start all over. God had
one nation out of all the nations on the earth, and He
told them, "Now if you will obey me, I'm going to have
a kingdom of priests." And they failed. The entire
nation of Israel did not want to be that committed, so
they developed the first clergy, the Levites. Instead of
all twelve tribes becoming a kingdom of priests, they
wound up with one tribe as priests, and it was not too
long until the whole thing fell apart because they
would not listen to God, nor would they obey! They
told Moses, "You go up there and talk to God, we'll stay
down here." So while Moses was with God receiving
the Ten Commandments, the Levites were busy
building a golden calf! And the "Levites" of today are
still doing the very same thing. We have golden calf
doctrines rather than hearing the voice of the Lord.

The Kingdom Promise to Joshua

Though the children of Israel would not enjoy what
had been promised to them, they would see glimpses of
what God intended to be theirs. Joshua is an excellent
example of God's intention for dominion authority for
His people. In Joshua 1:1 we read, "Now it came about
after the death of Moses the servant of the Lord that
the Lord spoke to Joshua the son of Nun, Moses'
servant, saying, 'Moses my servant is dead; now therefore arise, cross this Jordan, you and all this people, to
the land which I am giving to them, to the sons of
Israel. EVERY PLACE ON WHICH THE SOLE OF
YOUR FOOT TREADS, I HAVE GIVEN IT TO YOU,
JUST AS I SPOKE TO MOSES.'" Later in the passage
the Lord states, "For you shall give this people possession of the land which I swore to their fathers to give

them" (v. 6). This may be compared with Genesis 13:14, when God said, in effect, "Look at all this real estate. Look north, south, east, and west. See all this? I am going to give it to you and your seed and to your descendants forever." These words to Joshua marked the beginning of the fulfillment of that promise.

The Prophetic Witness — Jeremiah

Since God did not have a kingdom of priests, it was up to the prophets to keep alive the revelation of the purposes of God. Jeremiah was such a prophet. In Jeremiah 1:5-10 we read the following account of the call of this young prophet: " 'Before I formed you in the womb I knew you, and before you were born I consecrated you; I have appointed you a prophet to the nations.' Then I said, 'Alas, Lord God! Behold I do not know how to speak, because I am a youth.' But the Lord said to me, 'Do not say, "I am a youth," because everywhere I send you, you shall go, and all I command you, you shall speak. Do not be afraid of them, for I am with you to deliver you,' declares the Lord. Then the Lord stretched out His hand and touched my mouth, and the Lord said to me, 'Behold, I put My words in your mouth. See, I have appointed you this day over the nations and over the KINGDOMS'...'' This was not just Jeremiah's commission, but ours as well! If we have ears to hear and eyes to see, God is presently commissioning an awakening Church! As we approach the end of the twentieth century, we need to see OUR NAME there in that first chapter of Jeremiah! We need to read this promise as, "Then the Lord stretched out His hand and touched MY mouth, and said, 'Behold, I have put My words in YOUR mouth. I have appointed YOU this day over the nations and over the kingdoms.' "

Are we not to rule and reign with Christ as kings and priests? What is our commission? Exactly the same as Jeremiah's! That is confrontation. We are called, as Jeremiah was, to PLUCK UP, BREAK DOWN, DESTROY and to OVERTHROW. That is serious confrontation. Then God told Jeremiah that he was to "build and to plant." The Word declares that unless the Lord builds the house, they labor in vain that build it. There have been years of rubble (passivity) strewn through the Church. We have been waiting for years to strum our harps in heaven, and God is waiting for us to occupy on earth! Jeremiah received a word that was for nations and kingdoms.

The Prophetic Witness — Daniel

Jeremiah was not the only prophet receiving the Kingdom message. Daniel was another such prophet. Possibly more than any other Old Testament prophet, Daniel saw what God intended for His Kingdom. In Daniel chapter two, King Nebuchadnezzar had a dream that disturbed him greatly. He challenged his court magicians to interpret the dream without his telling them what the dream was. The magicians replied that this was impossible for any person other than God Himself. In frustration, King Nebuchadnezzar declared that all his court magicians, conjurers, and wise men in Babylon were to be executed. Even though Daniel and his friends were Jews, they were included in the king's edict. When they came to Daniel, he asked, "What's going on here?" And they explained the situation to Daniel. Since the wise men told the king that this was impossible, all of them were to be killed.

In Daniel 2:16-19 we read, "Daniel went in and requested of the king that he would give him time, in order that he might declare the interpretation to the king. Then Daniel went to his house and informed his friends, Hananiah, Mishael and Azariah, about the matter, in order that they might request compassion from the God of heaven concerning this mystery, so that Daniel and his friends might not be destroyed with the rest of the wise men of Babylon. Then the mystery was revealed to Daniel in a night vision. Then Daniel blessed the God of heaven...'' He went to the king and in verses 27-30 he explains, "As for the mystery about which the king has inquired, neither wise men, conjurers, magicians, nor diviners are able to declare it to the king. However, there is a God in heaven who reveals mysteries, and He has made known to King Nebuchadnezzar what will take place in the latter days. This was your dream and the visions in your mind while on your bed. As for you, O king, while on your bed your thoughts turned to what would take place in the future; and He who reveals mysteries has made known to you what will take place. But as for me, this mystery has not been revealed to me for any wisdom residing in me more than in any other living man, but for the purpose of making the interpretation known to the king, and that you may understand the thoughts of your mind.'' Daniel says that the dream concerns the future. It is our future as well.

Daniel describes the dream in verses 31-35: "You, O king, were looking and behold, there was a single great statue; that statue, which was large and of extra-ordinary splendor, was standing in front of you, and its appearance was awesome. The head of that statue was made of fine gold, its breast and its arms of silver, its belly and its thighs of bronze, its legs of iron, its feet partly of iron and partly of clay. You continued looking UNTIL A STONE WAS CUT OUT WITHOUT HANDS, and it struck the statue on its feet of iron and clay, and crushed them. Then the iron, the clay, the bronze, the silver and the gold were crushed all at the same time, and became like chaff from the summer threshing floors; and the wind carried them away so that not a trace of them was found. But the stone that struck the statue became a great mountain and filled the whole earth.''

Daniel continued to tell the king of these kingdoms that would come up after him. Then in verse 44 he concluded the vision and the interpretation of the dream, "And in the days of those kings the God of heaven will set up a kingdom which will never be destroyed, and that kingdom will not be left for another people; it will crush and put an end to ALL these kingdoms, but it will itself endure forever. Inasmuch as you saw that a stone was cut out of the mountain without hands and that it crushed the iron, the bronze, the clay, the silver, and the gold, the great God has made known to the king what will take place in the future; so the dream is true, and its interpretation is trustworthy.''

Daniel was a real man of God. The Lord gave him a very accurate picture of all human governments giving way to the Kingdom of God. Daniel had a clear understanding of the Kingdom of God. In fact, Daniel understood the Kingdom better than many Charismatics and Pentecostals today! Daniel said there would be a stone cut out of the mountain and it would crush, subdue and bring down every other kingdom ahead of it. He was foretelling of the kingdoms of man falling. That is why it was a stone that was cut out of the mountain without hands. This mountain, this Kingdom, is going to be the Kingdom that will subdue all of the things that man has done down through the ages, preying one on another. Right now we see kingdom divided against kingdom. We have had wars and heard rumors of wars. There is a restlessness upon the whole earth that has been initiated by God. He is getting ready to establish a Kingdom that will never end. Right now He is preparing a literal Kingdom to take over on the earth. It will crush, subdue and bring down every other kingdom raised up on the earth.

Daniel's Revelation Continues

Daniel continues to receive revelation about the Kingdom of God as we read in Daniel chapter seven (vv. 13-14). "I kept looking in the night visions, and behold, with the clouds of heaven one like a Son of Man was coming, and He came up to the Ancient of Days and was presented before Him. And to Him was given dominion, glory and a kingdom, that all the peoples, nations, and men of every language might serve Him. His dominion is an everlasting dominion which will not pass away; and His kingdom is one which will not be destroyed." Later, in verses 21 and 22, we read, "I kept looking, and that horn was waging war with the saints and overpowering them until the Ancient of Days came, and judgment was passed in favor of the saints of the Highest One, and the time arrived when the saints TOOK POSSESSION OF THE KINGDOM." Clearly, the time will come when the saints of the Highest One will possess what is theirs, which is the KINGDOM OF GOD.

It says in Daniel 7:18, "But the saints of the Highest One will receive the kingdom and possess the kingdom forever, for all ages to come." Then in verses 25-27, "And he [the beast] will speak out against the Most High and wear down the saints of the Highest One, and he will intend to make alterations in times and in law;

and they will be given into his hand for time, times, and half a time. But the court will sit for judgment, and his dominion will be taken away, annihilated and destroyed forever. Then the sovereignty, the dominion and the greatness of all the kingdoms under the whole heaven will be given to the people of the saints of the Highest One; His kingdom will be an everlasting kingdom, and all the dominions will serve and obey Him.''

This obviously has to do with the nations of the world. That is why the disciples' question was totally off base when they asked, "Wilt thou now restore the kingdom unto Israel?" Daniel's description of the Kingdom clearly states that all people are to be included, and that people of all nations and languages should serve Him! "His dominion is an everlasting dominion which shall not pass away, and His kingdom that which shall not be destroyed."

When Pilate came to Jesus and asked, "Are you the king?" Jesus answered, "Thou sayest." He kept pressing, and Jesus replied, "My kingdom is not of this world," *speaking of human governments.* Everyone tried to relate to Jesus on a natural plane. When we try to relate to spiritual things in the natural, we will never see what God is saying. It does not make sense because God's ways are so far above man's ways that we cannot grasp what God is saying.

Here Daniel is talking about God's Kingdom, which shall never be destroyed. Daniel 7:18 says, "But the saints of the Highest One will receive the kingdom and possess the kingdom forever, for all ages to come." How long is the Kingdom going to last? Forever! And it is for us to possess! Why is this so difficult to accept? Why is the vision of most people limited to getting to heaven so "they shall always be with the Lord"? We are constantly hearing people say, "Well, bless God, one of these days we're going to be over there." I'm sorry, but that is just songbook theology. The next item on the agenda is not for us to go "over there," because He is coming here. He is going to return to set up a Kingdom! Daniel 7:18 does not say, "And the time came when all the saints went to heaven." It says that the time came when the saints *possessed the Kingdom*. If we should die before Christ returns, there is no question that to be absent from the body is to be present with the Lord. We are not denying that. However, it is clear that when Christ returns He is bringing all the saints who have died back with Him. Why? Because He is going to set up His Kingdom!

The Time Is Coming!

We are in a climactic time in human history. It took 5,830 years from Adam to the year 1830 for the first billion people to come forth on this planet. It only took 100 years from 1830 to 1930 for the second billion. Only 31 years passed before the third billion, fifteen years for the fourth billion and just eleven years after that, in 1987, we had the fifth billion. The earth is being overwhelmed with people. There is no government on the face of the earth that is working properly. There is a restlessness among the heathen. There is a restlessness among those who know about God but have never submitted to Him. The world's financial markets are as stable as a feather in the wind. Everything is going to come down like dominoes.

In the midst of this turmoil, the people of God have hope and a message of hope — the Kingdom of God! In Hebrews 11:7, the Scripture gives an example in the person of Noah: "By faith Noah, being warned by God about things not yet seen, in reverence prepared an ark for the salvation of his household, by which HE condemned the world..." Who does it say condemned the world? Noah! All he was doing was following instructions. God repented that He made man and He gave Noah instructions about how to save his own family. Noah was the one who actually blew the whistle on the world of the ungodly.

Somewhere down the road it will be our job to blow the whistle on this generation. It cannot be done with vindictiveness. It cannot be done with any kind of personal feelings. Just as Daniel boldly proclaimed the Lord's intentions to the king, just as Noah lived by faith in obedience to God's will, we are going to see in the days to come a righteous, holy, mature people that will simply execute the judgments written. We do not make up those judgments, we merely execute them. Psalm 149:5-9 says, "Let the godly ones exult in glory; let them sing for joy on their beds. Let the high praises of God be in their mouth, and a two-edged sword in their hand, to execute vengeance on the nations, and punishment on the peoples; to bind their kings with chains, and their nobles with fetters of iron; to execute on them the judgment written; this is an honor for all His godly ones. Praise the Lord!" The job of the saints is to execute the Lord's judgments. God is raising up an army.

The Lord did it once before. At the flood He cleaned house. Who was left after the flood? Noah and his family — the righteous. Malachi 3:1 says, " 'Behold, I am going to send My messenger, and he will clear the way before Me. And the Lord, whom you seek, will suddenly come to His temple; and the messenger of the covenant, in whom you delight, behold, He is coming,' says the Lord of hosts." This was speaking prophetically of John the Baptist, who would come and "prepare the way of the Lord." He was that voice in the wilderness. Right now the wind of the Spirit is blowing! A John the Baptist company is being raised up right now. There is a trumpet being sounded by many voices with the same message. We are at the change of an age. We are going to see the most dramatic changes that have ever come about in the history of the world, the Church, and among nations within the next few years! Are we ready? Are we preparing the way?

Getting the Church Ready

"But who can endure the day of His coming?" (Mal. 3:2) Note that expression, "the day of His coming." Zephaniah talks about the day of the Lord 21 times in three chapters. The Book of Joel mentions the day of the Lord 18 times in three chapters. Every time we see that term, it speaks of a day of darkness, a day of gloom, which refers to the wicked. However, Jesus said the righteous should lift up their heads and rejoice because they know that their redemption is near. Malachi 3:2 continues, "But who can endure the day of His coming? And who can stand when He appears? For He is like a refiner's fire and like fullers' soap." Not too many people today know that fullers' soap was made mostly out of lye. God is getting ready to clean up the Church. Even if He has to take a little hide off, He is going to get a squeaky clean Church.

Malachi continues: " '...and He will sit as a smelter and purifier of silver, and He will purify the sons of Levi and refine them like gold and silver, so that they may present to the Lord offerings in righteousness. Then the offerings of Judah and Jerusalem will be pleasing to the Lord, as in the days of old and as in former years. Then I will draw near to you for judgment; and I will be a swift witness against the sorcerers and against the adulterers and against those who swear falsely, and against those who oppress the wage earner and his wages, the widow and the orphan, and those who turn aside the alien, and do not fear Me,' says the Lord of hosts" (Mal. 3:2-5).

What the Lord is telling us in the passage is that anything that is out of order, anything that is evil, wicked, or deceptive God will deal with. The Word says He will be a "swift witness against sorcerers" or anything involving witchcraft. He will be a swift witness against the adulterers. We live in a promiscuous age. People justify anything they want to do. But God is going to deal with it. We have heard a lot lately about "safe sex," but there is no such thing as "safe sin." The Bible says that the soul that sins shall surely die! The righteous should not fear, but the unrighteous are in trouble.

We must know that the Kingdom of God is a LIFESTYLE before we can understand any other part of it. Technically, it is immaterial WHEN the Lord comes. It does not matter whether we go through the tribulation or whether we are raptured out. But we must understand that if we are going to be a part of these days ahead of us, we are going to have to live clean or we will not be a part of anything God is doing. The key is righteousness, peace and joy. Paul, in Romans 14:17 said "...for the kingdom of God is not eating and drinking, but righteousness and peace and joy in the Holy Spirit." This is what the Kingdom of God is all about — a lifestyle unto God.

Continuing on in Malachi chapter three, verse 16, we read "Then those who feared the Lord spoke to one another, and the Lord gave attention and heard it, and a book of remembrance was written before Him for those who fear the Lord and who esteem His name.

'And they [those that fear Him] will be Mine,' says the Lord of hosts, 'on the day that I prepare My own possession, and I will spare them as a man spares his own son who serves him.' " He is speaking here of the righteous. "So you will AGAIN distinguish between the righteous and the wicked, between one who serves God and one who does not serve Him" (v. 18). What the Word is telling us is that as God distinguished between the righteous and the wicked during the days of Noah, so will He once again on that day of His glorious return.

When the Lord returns He is going to judge the ungodly. Many of us have been taught that He is going to have to somehow rescue the pathetic, passive, whining Church, because things are going to be so bad He is going to have to have a special sneak program to get us out. Yet that is not God's agenda! He took care of the children of Israel when all those plagues were falling on Egypt. He took care of all those rebels for 40 years while they were crying in the wilderness. He did not even let their shoes wear out. He put spigots on rocks. He babysat them while they were constantly fussing at Him. If He was that good to that bunch of rebellious people, can He not take care of us now regardless of what takes place upon the earth?

The Prophetic Witness — Isaiah

Let us keep this straight...God is for His people and His people are going to establish His Kingdom on this earth. The unrighteous have no part in it. Isaiah was another prophet who saw clearly the message of the Kingdom of God. Let's look at a very familiar passage, Isaiah 9:6 (using both the *King James Version* and the *New American Standard Version*). "For unto us a child is born. Unto us a son is given. And the government shall be upon His shoulders. And His name shall be called Wonderful, Counselor, the Mighty God, the Everlasting Father, the Prince of Peace. Of the increase of His government and peace, there shall be no end, upon the throne of David and upon His kingdom, to order it and to establish it with judgment and with justice, from henceforth, even forever. The zeal of the Lord will perform this.'' Isaiah prophesied this 714 years before Jesus was even born! In this passage he foretold the birth and the government and Kingdom that would be established by the Lord Jesus.

The prophets were constantly talking about the Kingdom that Jesus would establish that would never, never end. Remember, this was one of the primary questions in the disciples' minds when Jesus got ready to ascend to heaven after the resurrection, because THEY KNEW THE OLD TESTAMENT PROPHECIES. They knew what those prophets had to say about the Kingdom that was coming. The Book of Isaiah is filled with these prophecies. In Isaiah 29:17-19 he wrote, ''Is it not yet just a little while before Lebanon will be turned into a fertile field, and the fertile field will be considered as a forest? And on that day the deaf shall hear the words of a book, and out of their gloom and darkness the eyes of the blind shall see. The afflicted also shall increase their gladness in the Lord, and the needy of mankind shall rejoice in the Holy One of Israel.'' How is this to take place? Verse 20 explains, ''For the ruthless will come to an end, and the scorner will be finished, indeed all who are intent on doing evil will be CUT OFF...''

The prophet continues in chapter 33 of Isaiah, beginning with verse 13, '' 'You who are far away, hear what I have done; and you who are near, acknowledge My might.' Sinners in Zion are terrified; Trembling has seized the godless. Who among us can live with the consuming fire? [This ties in with Malachi, dealing with the refiner's fire.] Who among us can live with continual burning?" Who indeed? Verse 15 gives the answer, "He who walks righteously, and speaks with sincerity, he who rejects unjust gain, and shakes his hands so that they hold no bribe; he who stops his ears from hearing about bloodshed, and shuts his eyes from looking upon evil; he will dwell on the heights; His refuge will be the impregnable rock; His bread will be given him; His water will be sure. Your eyes will see the King in His beauty; They will behold a far-distant land." If we walk righteously, we do not have a thing to fear! Our immunity is in obedience! Our immunity is in our relationship to the King.

This principle is what kingdom now theology is all about. It does not matter what comes on the earth. He is our High Tower! He is our Rock of refuge! That is the blessing that comes to those who walk circumspectly before the Lord. The Old Testament prophets were pointing to something. Now we will begin to look at the One who came, not just to point to the Kingdom, but to live it — Jesus.

CHAPTER FOUR

The Gospel of the Kingdom

World Evangelization

We are now going to consider one of the most important and perhaps most misunderstood terms in the Bible, "the gospel of the Kingdom." Jesus spoke of the importance of this message in Matthew 24:14, "And this gospel of the kingdom shall be preached in the whole world for a witness to all the nations, and then the end shall come." There are two great misunderstandings about the gospel of the Kingdom. The first is the idea that this passage is the same as the Great Commission passage of Matthew 28:19, "Go therefore and make disciples of all nations, baptizing them in the name of the Father, and the Son and the Holy Spirit..." Because both passages use the phrase "all nations," many have assumed that they are both speaking of the same thing. The other misunderstanding is the concept that the gospel of the Kingdom is the same as the gospel of salvation. Because of these faulty ideas, many believers have not grasped the message of the Kingdom of God.

The traditional view has been that when everybody has heard about Jesus, then He would return. This has been taught so long and by so many that we naturally assume it to be true. It WOULD be true if Jesus had said in Matthew 24 that the gospel of salvation needed to be preached to all nations for the end to come. But that is not what He said. He said the gospel of the KINGDOM shall be preached, and then the end shall come. We know that these are not the same thing because THE WHOLE WORLD WAS EVANGELIZED IN THE FIRST CENTURY, yet Jesus did not return.

Look at Acts 2:1-5. "And when the day of Pentecost had come, they were all together in one place. And suddenly there came from heaven a noise like a violent, rushing wind, and it filled the whole house where they were sitting. And there appeared to them tongues as of fire distributing themselves, and they rested on each one of them. And they were all filled with the Holy Spirit and began to speak with other tongues, as the Spirit was giving them utterance. Now there were Jews living in Jerusalem, devout men, from every nation under heaven." According to God's Word, every nation under heaven was represented in Jerusalem on the Day of Pentecost when these three thousand men, besides women and children, were saved. They were there celebrating the Feast of Pentecost and they had come from all over the world for that event. Verse 6 goes on to say, "And when this sound occurred, the multitude came together, and were bewildered, because they were each one hearing them speak in his own language." They could not understand how Galileans could speak the languages of the nations that they had come from, so obviously they were from many different countries.

Could that phrase, "every nation under heaven,"

just be an expression? No, because verses 9 and 10 even list the different nationalities that were represented. For example, it mentions Elamites. The Elamites were descendants of Noah's grandson through Shem. These people settled in the Persian Gulf area and for many, many centuries they were called Persians. When the Shah took over the country in 1934, they changed the name of the country to Iran. So on the Day of Pentecost there were a whole group of Iranian Jews who got saved! We know from Church history also that Bartholomew, one of the original twelve apostles, spent his entire life in Iran ministering to the Iranians.

The Iranians have been evangelized. They threw Christianity out over fourteen centuries ago. We have had the mistaken notion that Jesus cannot return until we go back to each nation, like Iran, and repreach the gospel to them. But they had the gospel and they got rid of it. It was an Iranian king, King Cyrus, who rebuilt the temple for the Jews. It was an Iranian king that Esther married. When Mordecai and Esther found out about the plot that Haman had conceived to kill all the Jews, it was King Xerxes who spared them. They were Iranian kings that went to Herod and asked, "Where is he who is born king of the Jews?" Those kings of the east were from Persia, present-day Iran. Iran has been given the gospel of salvation.

The same is true of the Jews. Jesus came to His own and they did not receive Him. That is why Jesus stood outside Jerusalem and said, "O Jerusalem, Jerusalem, who kills the prophets and stones those who are sent to her! How often I wanted to gather your children together, the way a hen gathers her chicks under her wings, and you were unwilling" (Matt. 23:37). He grieved over the city and said, "You did not know your hour of visitation." The Jews broke their covenant with God. He was the Stone the builders rejected. This does not mean, of course, that we do not do everything that we can to win the Jews and the Iranians to Christ. We are only trying to make the point that if all that was necessary for Jesus to return was for each nation to have a witness of Christ, then Jesus would have returned in the first century, right after the Day of Pentecost. There are four passages of Scripture that show that the whole world was evangelized in the first century; Acts 2:5, Romans 10:14-21, Colossians 1:3-6, and Colossians 1:23. Obviously, the "gospel of the Kingdom" must mean something other than the "gospel of salvation."

The Gospel of the Kingdom

What did Jesus mean by the "gospel of the King-dom"? Let's look at an example in Luke 19, His encounter with the man Zaccheus. It says in verse 1, "And He entered and was passing through Jericho. And behold, there was a man called by the name of Zaccheus; and he was a chief tax-gatherer, and he was rich. And he was trying to see who Jesus was, and he was unable because of the crowd, for he was small in stature. And he ran on ahead and climbed up into a sycamore tree in order to see Him, for He was about to pass through that way. And when Jesus came to the place, He looked up and said to him, 'Zaccheus, hurry and come down, for today I must stay at your house.' And he hurried and came down, and received Him gladly. And when they saw it, they all began to grumble, saying, 'He has gone to be the guest of a man who is a sinner.' And Zaccheus stopped and said to the Lord, 'Behold, Lord, half of my possessions I will give to the poor, and if I have defrauded anyone of anything, I will give back four times as much.' And Jesus said to him, 'Today salvation has come to this house, because he, too, is a son of Abraham. For the Son of Man has come to seek and to save that which was lost.' " The very next verse says, "And while they were listening to these things, He went on to tell a parable, because he was near Jerusalem, and they supposed that the kingdom of God was going to appear immediately."

There it is again, "the kingdom of God." When Jesus began His ministry, when John the Baptist began his ministry, when Jesus commissioned the twelve disciples in Matthew 10 and told them to go out and preach the gospel, when He sent the 70 out two by two — in every instance the first words that came out of their mouths were, "The kingdom of heaven is at hand." Not once did He instruct them, "Tell people to get ready for heaven." Jesus said, "The kingdom of heaven is at hand." This is a powerful message. He pulls a short man named Zaccheus out of a tree, and in their discourse this man completely changes the direction of his life. Suddenly, the things that Zaccheus had been living for were not as important as they had been. He sees the lifestyle that he has been living as corrupt, and he is going to make it right. Incredibly, those who were observing all this became disturbed! They wondered if the Kingdom of God was going to appear immediately because Jesus had been teaching about it as being at hand. All they had been hearing about was the Kingdom. The disciples had been talking about the Kingdom, John the Baptist had been talking about the Kingdom — so the people are asking, "Where is it?"

Parables of the Kingdom

Many Christians today are asking the same question. But Jesus told His disciples that it does not come with observation, but that it is within us (Luke 17:20). So how does the Kingdom of God come? Can we see it? Can we touch it? No, because it is mystical, it comes without observation. This is very unsatisfying to our soulish selves. We live on such a sensual level; what we can see, what we can taste, what we can handle, what we can understand. It has to make sense. Yet the Kingdom of God comes without observation. We cannot say, "Here it is; there it is." It is illusive to logic.

Jesus answered the question with a parable, beginning with verse 12 of Luke 19.

'A certain nobleman went to a distant country to receive a kingdom for himself, and then return. And he called ten of his slaves, and gave them ten minas, and said to them, "Do business with this until I come back." ' But his citizens hated him, and sent a delegation after him, saying, "We do not want this man to reign over us." And it came about that when he returned, after receiving the kingdom, he ordered that these slaves, to whom he had given the money, be called to him in order that he might know what business they had done. And the first appeared, saying, "Master, your mina has made ten minas more." And he said to him, "Well done, good slave, because you have been faithful in a very little thing, be in authority over ten cities." [Take note of that! This slave had been faithful in a little and now he was placed in authority over ten cities. The Lord rewards faithfulness.]

The parable continues with the second slave, 'And the second came saying, "Your mina, master, has made five minas." And he said to him also, "And you are to be over five cities." And another came, saying, "Master, behold your mina which I kept put away in a handkerchief; for I was afraid of you, because you are an exacting man; you take up what you did not lay down, and reap what you did not sow." He said to him, "By your own words I will judge you, you worthless slave. Did you know that I am an exacting man, taking up what I did not lay down and reaping what I did not sow? Then why did you not put the money in the bank, and having come, I would have collected it with interest?" And he said to the bystanders, "Take the mina away from him, and give it to the one who has the ten minas." And they said to him, "Master, he has ten minas already." ' Now Jesus drives the point of the parable home in verse 26, 'I tell you, that to everyone who has shall more be given, but from the one who does not have, even what he does have shall be taken away.' "

Does this parable seem a little cold? It really is not. When Jesus gives us something, He wants us to take what He gives us and cherish it and be diligent. The parable speaks in terms of minas, but it is really referring to spiritual principles. When we are faithful with our "minas," the reward is to rule ten cities, five cities, whatever. The reward of unfaithfulness is no cities! To whom much is given, much is required.

Jesus tells another parable in Matthew chapter 13 that ties right back into this parable in Luke 19. In Matthew 13 Jesus delivers the parable of the sower. In verses 10-16 it says, "And the disciples came and said to Him, 'Why do you speak to them in parables?' And He answered and said to them, 'To you it has been granted to know the mysteries of the kingdom of heaven, but to them it has not been granted. For whoever has, to him shall more be given, and he shall have an abundance; but whoever does not have, even what he has shall be taken away from him. Therefore, I speak to them in parables; because while seeing they do not see, and while hearing they do not hear, nor do they understand. And in their case the prophecy of Isaiah is being fulfilled, which says, *"You will keep on hearing, but will not understand; and you will keep on seeing, but will not perceive; for the heart of this people has become dull, and with their ears they scarcely hear, and they have closed their eyes lest they should see with their eyes, and hear with their ears, and under-stand with their heart and return, and I should heal them."* *"But blessed are your eyes* [speaking to the twelve disciples] *because they see; and your ears, because they hear.* Verse 19: *"When anyone hears the WORD OF THE KINGDOM, and does not understand it, the evil one comes and snatches away what has been sown in his heart..."*

It is very important for the body of Christ to understand why we are here on this planet. God wants us to be blessed. He wants us to walk in health. He wants us to be emotionally sound, and to walk together in love. There are a lot of things that God wants us to have. But do we know why? Why are we to be well? Why are we to walk in victory? Why are we to be filled with the Spirit, walk in the Spirit, and be led by the Spirit? Why does God want us to understand these things? SO THAT WHEN THE LORD RETURNS, WE WILL BE WITHOUT SPOT OR WRINKLE AND WILL BE SPIRITUALLY EQUIPPED TO RULE AND REIGN WITH CHRIST FOR ALL AGES TO COME!

Can we receive this message of the gospel of the Kingdom? God wants us to be healed, but there is more to serving Him than getting healed. God wants us to be well, He wants us to be filled with the Spirit, He wants us to be blessed and prosperous and all of that. But it leads to something. Jesus taught His disciples to pray, "Thy kingdom come, thy will be done on earth as it is in heaven." God's purpose is to see His will accomplished here as it is in heaven. Many people's concept of serving God is simply going to heaven, and "so shall we always be with the Lord." How shallow! God wants us to see that He desires that the saints possess the Kingdom!

Possessing the Promises

The moment we are saved we are born into the Kingdom of God. But there comes a time in the future when the saints will possess the Kingdom literally. The moment we are born again we are translated from the kingdom of darkness into the kingdom of His dear Son. However, the greatest event is just ahead of us, when the saints literally possess the Kingdom. Through Jesus Christ we are able to come into those promises and prophecies that were spoken to Abraham, Moses, Daniel, Isaiah and all the rest. These were summed up in Jesus' words in Matthew 5:5 — "The meek...shall inherit the earth." He was restating what God said to Abram in Genesis 13:15 when He told Abram to look in ALL directions...north, south, east and west. Then, after Abram had gazed at all of that "real estate," God made him a promise. God said, "I am going to GIVE to you and your descendants ALL of the LAND FOREVER." When Jesus said in Matthew 5:5, "Blessed are the meek, for they shall inherit the earth," He was CONFIRMING God's promise to Abram AND TO HIS DESCENDANTS! And that means *us*!

The key to understanding the Kingdom of God is to see how that promise to Abram was fulfilled. It was about 600 years after God gave this promise to Abram that Joshua and the children of Israel got one square foot of land. They had to "take possession" of the promise. Let us go back to the Book of Joshua and notice how this happened. "Now it came about after the death of Moses the servant of the Lord that the Lord spoke to Joshua the son of Nun, Moses' servant, saying, 'Moses My servant is dead; now therefore arise, cross this Jordan, you and all this people, to the land which I am giving to them, to the sons of Israel. Every place on which the sole of your foot treads, I have given it to you, just as I spoke to Moses' " (Josh. 1:1-3). The Lord goes on to describe the land that they are to receive. Then in verse 5 the Lord tells Joshua, "No man will be able to stand before you all the days of your life. Just as I have been with Moses, I will be with you; I will not fail you or forsake you. Be strong and courageous, for you shall give this people possession of the land which I swore to their fathers to give them." This refers to Genesis chapter thirteen and God's promise of giving the land to Abram and his descendants. The promise is about to be fulfilled.

Then in Joshua chapter three, we read, "Then Joshua rose early in the morning; and he and all the sons of Israel set out from Shittim and came to the Jordan, and they lodged there before they crossed. And it came about at the end of three days that the officers went through the midst of the camp; and they commanded the people, saying, 'When you see the ark of the covenant of the Lord your God with the Levitical priests carrying it, then you shall set out from your place and go after it.' " Here a principle is laid out for us. When we see the ark we are to follow it. It is not complicated. When we see the cloud, move with it. When the ark of anointing begins to pass by, get up and start moving.

Jericho Must Go

Joshua can teach us much about the principle of possession. There is something required of God's people to receive the promised Kingdom. In Genesis 13 when God tells Abram He is going to give him all the land, He did not tell him that his descendants, the children of Israel, under the leadership of Joshua, would have to subdue 31 nations to get the "gift" of all that land that had been promised. We are told that the meek shall inherit the earth, but that we must press in to take it. Matthew 11:12 says, "...the Kingdom of heaven suffers violence, and violent men take it by force." We have to see it and then go after it. We must understand what it is all about. Joshua was told by the Lord in Joshua 6:2, "...See, I have given Jericho into your hand..." Back in those days there were walls built around cities. The walls of the city of Jericho were so wide that they could race chariots side by side. The whole army of Jericho is up there on the wall, along with the king, looking down at the people of Israel. God tells Joshua, "See this city?" And Joshua says, "Uh huh." God says, "I've given it to you." Joshua replies, "Oh!" He looks up and sees the whole army of Jericho looking down on him from those impregnable walls. God tells him, "I HAVE given you this city."

Any time God says, "I am going to give you something," we need to raise our eyebrows, because there is a hook somewhere. In this case, it was a simple act of obedience. God said, "Now here's the strategy; I want you to put an armed guard in front of the ark, and seven priests carrying seven trumpets before the ark, and put an armed guard behind the ark. You are going to have the priests blowing trumpets, you are going to have the armed guard followed by the ark, then behind that will be another armed guard, followed by all the mass of Israel bringing up the rear. You are to go around the city once each day for seven days, and on the seventh day you are to surround the city seven times. In this battle maneuver, Joshua, all you are supposed to do is walk and stare at the city. THERE IS TO BE NO DISCUSSION OR CONVERSATION ABOUT IT. KEEP YOUR MOUTHS SHUT FOR A CHANGE!''

Imagine us going 24 hours without uttering a word. Easy? Try fasting negative words for a day sometime. God was trying to get a message across to His people. He was telling them, "This time there will be no talking.'' Forty years earlier they had sent spies into this same land. They came back with a "grasshopper mentality'' — they saw the enemy and from that perspective they became grasshoppers. As a result, they were unable to take the land. So now God tells them, "This time around we are not going to discuss whether we can or cannot. Just do what I say for a change!''

So they marched around the city. This is one of the most amazing stories in the Bible. Three million Jews walking around Jericho with nobody talking. There are seven priests out there tooting on trumpets to make sure everybody in the city is watching. So the inhabitants of Jericho look out and all they see are three million people silently staring at them! That first day they must have thought that these Israelites were crazy. And to top it off, there was this armed guard around a funny looking box (the ark). The residents of Jericho had to be wondering, "What is in that box?''

Picture the scene — if we had one person walking back and forth in front of our house for just twenty minutes staring at it, we would be on the phone to the cops! See what God is doing? By this strange strategy,

God has psyched out a whole nation. A boxer knows how to psyche out his opponent. If the weaker opponent can psyche his opponent into thinking that he is going to knock his block off, the stronger guy begins to get nervous and becomes vulnerable. Then his guard goes down and he loses the fight.

The Earth Is Ours

We need to realize that the earth is ours. We have been the ones who have been psyched into thinking it is not! What does the Word of God have to say? Proverbs 13:22 says, "...The wealth of the sinner is stored up for the righteous." Zephaniah 1:13 promises "...they [those "stagnant of Spirit"] will build houses but not inhabit them, and plant vineyards but not drink their wine." Who are the ones to inherit those vineyards and houses? This generation of Christians must wake up to the fact that the only way we will be a part of this grand finale is to have an overcoming walk with God! We will not be able to be a part of this Kingdom by just memorizing a few verses of Scripture and trying to use them like a rabbit's foot! It will take a lot more than wearing a big phylactery on the forehead to "inherit the earth." It will take a lot more than religious symbols. We can carry a cross as big as our body, but if we are not walking with God, we will be excluded from His holy Kingdom!

There is a promise, but there is also possession. Jesus told His disciples, "Do not be afraid, little flock, for your Father has chosen gladly to give you the kingdom" (Luke 12:32) (so far so good), but Acts 14:22 says, "...through many tribulations we must enter the kingdom of God." Thanks a lot, Lord. You mean we have to take it? Yes, that is exactly what He means. We all want the blessings, but we want no responsibility.

We have been so immersed in our comfort-oriented society that we have developed a passivity as it concerns the Kingdom. Jesus told His disciples that it was the "violent" who would take the Kingdom (Matt. 11:12). Unfortunately, we do not have too many people who want to be violent. They would rather sit in their rapture rockers and reach for the blast-off button!

David learned a lot about spiritual warfare the day he stood out in the valley and listened to Goliath taunting the army of Israel. There must be a violence that rises up inside of us to throw off the restraints of the spirit of this age as did David in his day. David had no problem with the size of Goliath. He simply saw somebody who did not have a blood covenant. David looked at his own brothers who were soldiers in the army of God, and he looked at the giant, and all he saw was an uncircumcised Philistine. He knew before he ever threw that stone that anyone without a covenant had no protection. We are people of covenant! We are the ones who will walk through any problem. We have covenant protection. God does not save by many, He saves by obedience. He said the meek shall inherit the earth, and we SHALL inherit it. He would never have told Abraham, Isaac and Jacob that He would give to them and their descendants ALL THE LAND FOREVER...and then have them "disappear."

Taking the Kingdom by Force

There is some warfare involved in serving God. There has to be a violence in our spirits. "The kingdom of heaven suffereth violence, and violent men take it by force." Satan is the intimidator. He usurps and he tries to keep us oppressed and restrained. But once we break through those walls of restraint and stand up and prophesy the Word of the Lord, then we are loosed from restraints that satan tries to bring upon us. We must be violent in our spirits against the spirit of this age. We must rise up in violence, because satan would like to keep us asleep — just go in, sing a few songs; hear a nice little word; go home and go to work the next day; maybe pray a few minutes or think about the Lord a little bit every day. But we need violence in our spirits constantly! We determine that we are not going to be intimidated for one minute or one second of any day. But when the evil one comes to us, we say, "Satan, get out of here, you liar." Begin by prophesying the word of the Lord into your own spirit. Say, "I prophesy release to my spirit this day and I am going to walk in victory." Be violent in your spirit every day! We do not give satan one inch of territory! This KINGDOM is going to come forth — and we need to take possession violently!

We are not doing this on our own, however. Being violent does not mean that we can grab hold of our own boot straps. We are not going to possess the Kingdom by some good works or screaming or hollering. Being violent has to do with an intensity of spirit to see the purposes of God fulfilled — those which the Scriptures foretell! When we have a promise that says that the saints will possess the Kingdom, we do not just passively sit down and say, "Bless me, O God. Bless me, O God. Bless me, O God" again and again and again. The whole purpose of being blessed and claiming everything that God has for us is to prepare us for the war we are in, to dispossess the god of this world who is the usurper of OUR PROPERTY! When we grasp this revelation, we will get past the daydreaming mentality of just getting to heaven. The next event on God's calendar is NOT going to heaven! This next step is to set up His Kingdom and to cause the meek to inherit the earth. We, His saints, are to rule and reign with Him as kings and priests forever.

What do we really want? Would we really rather go to heaven, or help usher in the Kingdom? Daniel 7:22 says "...and the time arrived when the saints took possession of the kingdom." Paul wrote to the Romans in chapter 16, verse 20, "And the God of peace will soon crush Satan under YOUR feet." We cannot be timid about promises like these! If the Lord is going to crush satan under our feet, then we do not want to be playing pattycake somewhere. We should get involved. We should want to pay a little pay back to the devil, who has buffeted us for years. We finally get a chance to help put him in his place. God has an issue to settle with satan, and we are going to be around to help Him settle it.

CHAPTER FIVE

The Kingdom Message for the Church

Getting Past First Base

What do we do with the message of the gospel of the Kingdom? Let us go to the Book of Hebrews and examine what God expects from His people. "Concerning him [Melchizedek] we have much to say, and it is hard to explain, since you have become dull of hearing. For though by this time you ought to be teachers, you have need again for someone to teach you the elementary principles of the oracles of God, and you have come to need milk and not solid food. For everyone who partakes only of milk is not accustomed to the word of righteousness, for he is a babe. But solid food is for the mature, who because of practice have their senses trained to discern good and evil" (Heb. 5:11-14). Even though chapter five ends right here, we should remember that the Bible was not divided into chapters until about 700 years ago. The first word of chapter 6 is "therefore". The "therefore" refers to what we just read. It says, "Therefore LEAVING the elementary teaching about the Christ, let us press on to maturity, NOT laying again a foundation of repentance from dead works and of faith toward God, of instruction about washings, and laying on of hands, and the resurrection of the dead, and eternal judgment. And this we shall do, if God permits" (vv. 1-3).

A modern paraphrase of this last verse could be, "And this we shall do if we can get the nipple and bottle out of our mouths." How many times do we have to lay the foundation? How many times do we have to be taught about the authority of the believer? How many times do we have to be told about laying hands on the sick or the resurrection from the dead? All of these teachings are basic. We need to lay hold of the message of the Kingdom. We need to start to grow up.

Jesus explained it so perfectly when He said, "When anyone hears the word of the kingdom and does not understand it, the evil one comes and snatches away what has been sown in his heart." A lot of people have given their hearts to Christ. But they never laid hold of what the purpose or God's plan was. The Kingdom of God is more than just escaping hell. The Kingdom of God is more than praying for healing or getting our needs met or having our finances taken care of. According to Second Peter 1:3, God HAS granted to us everything that pertains to life and godliness. But He has an overall plan. It is to point us to the Kingdom.

The Third Call

The first presentation of the Kingdom was given to Moses in Exodus. God told Moses to tell the people of Israel, "Now then, if you will indeed obey My voice and keep My covenant, then you shall be My own possession among all the peoples, for all the earth is

MINE" (Ex. 19:5). God lays claim to the earth. It does NOT belong to the devil. Then the Lord continues, "...And you shall be to me a KINGDOM OF PRIESTS AND A HOLY NATION" (v.6). God wanted all twelve tribes to be priestly. His first plan was that all of Israel would be a Kingdom of priests unto Him. But the Israelites said, "No, we can't handle that. You go talk to God, Moses. If God speaks to us, we will die" (Ex. 20:19, paraphrase).

So the second choice was that the Levites would be the priests. One tribe, the tribe of Levi, served as the substitute priesthood. But they perverted the Old Testament law and by the time Jesus arrived, they were in the front of the crowd yelling, "Crucify Him, crucify Him." Jesus again offered the promise of the Kingdom to the nation of Israel, but they still rejected it. The first call was in Exodus, the second call was in the gospels. They rejected the King, and thus His realm.

We are now in the third presentation of the Kingdom. How much will this generation see? Jesus said, "And this gospel of the kingdom shall be preached in the whole world for a witness to all the nations, and then the end shall come" (Matt. 24:14). For almost six thousand years God has been waiting for someone who can hear what He is really saying! Very few people in any age initially hear what God is saying. But God ALWAYS has a man!

During the first 1,656 years, a time period from Adam to the flood, there were only three people who, according to Scripture, walked with God: Adam, Enoch, and Noah. It took God another 427 years after the flood to find a fourth man that He could talk to. His name was Abram. From Adam to Abram (or from the FALL to the CALL) 2,083 years passed, during which time God found four people to whom He could relate. Now

God is once again speaking of His Kingdom to this last generation. Once again He is presenting His eternal purposes through many voices with the prophetic intensity of John the Baptist who heralded His coming the first time so many years ago! How many people in the Church today will be able to hear His voice through His anointed vessels who are commissioned by Him to "prepare the way of the Lord" for the establishment of HIS GLORIOUS KINGDOM ON EARTH...AS IT IS IN HEAVEN?

Growing Up and Going On

When we begin to see what the Word is really saying, we will realize that the entire Bible is a handbook concerning dominion theology. We are the people of God, the holy nation, the royal priesthood to whom God has given the keys of the Kingdom. Jesus told Peter that whatever things HE would bind would be bound. That was a Kingdom promise! Jesus told Peter that whatever things HE would loose would be loosed. Jesus was looking for that man who would believe the Kingdom promises. He has given us the authority. He has given us the anointing. We are not only to believe the Word, but also to walk in it. When we begin to lay hold of that Word and to walk in it, no weapon that is formed against us can prosper!

The Church has been hindered because it is not getting beyond the elementary principles! We start out as babes, but we are not to stay there. There are four stages of growth and development in the life of the believer. The first stage is listed in First Corinthians 3:1-3, where we are described as babes who desire the sincere milk of the Word. The second stage is that of little children, mentioned in First John 2:1 — "My little children, I am writing these things to you that you may not sin. And if anyone sins, we have an Advocate with the Father, Jesus Christ the righteous.'' The third stage of growth and development is as young men. First John 2:13 describes young men who have overcome the evil one. Finally, the fourth stage is that of "sons," mentioned in Romans 8:14. These are those who, by the Spirit, ARE the sons of God.

All creation, according to Romans chapter 8, is groaning in travail, waiting for the manifestation of the sons of God to come forth. What does that mean? God Himself, and all of creation, is waiting for the Church to grow up. He is waiting for us to become mature. This does not mean He wants some select, holier-than-thou, judgmental group who cuts each other up with their pet doctrines. God is looking for people to grow up. This is what the writer to the Hebrews was saying in Hebrews 6:1. "Therefore LEAVING the elementary teaching about the Christ, let us press on to maturity..." not laying down the basics over and over and over. Any building only needs one foundation. How many times can a foundation be laid before something is built upon it?

Foundational Ministries

At a luncheon recently we had a number of pastors present, and we were specifically dealing with the foundational ministries of apostles and prophets. We were discussing their role, function, and purpose. I stated that we have not had the functional foundational ministries of apostles and prophets for virtually 1700 years, but that God is now restoring those two ministries to the Church. This was an important message to these men and women. For so long some have had a tendency to take the vessel and try to elevate him up on some kind of a pedestal and say, "Oh, he's an apostle," "she's a prophet."

This is the hour when God is establishing the foundation of the Church, but the purpose of the foundational ministries, along with evangelists, pastors and teachers, is to equip the saints for the work of service, that we grow up and come into the unity of the faith. When Jesus ascended to heaven, it states in Ephesians 4:13 that "He gave gifts unto men." These gifts are what we term the five-fold ministries. Consider that word "gave" for a moment. In the Greek language, that word GAVE is in the aorist tense, which denotes continuous action. If we read it in English the way it reads in Greek, it would say, "He gave, is giving, and will give, some as apostles, some as prophets, some as evangelists, some as pastors and teachers." It is happening now!

God is restoring the foundational ministries of apostles and prophets in these last days, but it will not be a fanfare ministry. There will be no Hollywood publicity with trumpets and bright lights flashing as the curtain is pulled back. The key word is "foundation." If we went to Washington D.C. and saw the United States Capitol or the Washington Monument, we would not run up and say, "Oh look at the beautiful foundation!" Of course not; we are not even cognizant of it. We would simply stand in awe of the beautiful structure that rests on the foundation.

This explains what has been wrong with the Church. Lacking functional foundational ministries of apostles and prophets, the Church has been lopsided for centuries! That is why we have had 20,000 groups fighting each other, each saying, "We have the truth!" (That is a true statistic, by the way. We had 900 denominations in 1950 and that number has continued to grow each year, to 20,000 as of the last statistical count in 1985.) What God is after is a holy habitation of lively stones. As the foundation is restored to the Church, God will give correction where there has been error and distortion. God will rectify all things. We are going to see this holy habitation of God come forth on the proper foundation. We will not be cognizant of personalities because all of our eyes are going to be turned toward what the Spirit is doing in our lives. God is bringing forth this end-time Kingdom of priests, this holy nation, this army that Joel so vividly described in chapter two that would rise up in the last days. There has to come a time when the suspicion and the questioning of one another's motives comes to an end.

Sometime we have to grow up. As we come into the fulness of the measure of the stature of Christ, as God begins to restore order through the authority of the apostle and the wisdom of the prophet, we are going to see the structure coming back to be what God intended it to be. When Jesus told Peter, "The gates of hell shall not prevail against the Church," that is exactly what He meant! It does not matter what it looks like now. God IS in control. God has been God for a long time, and He has had lots of practice. He knows exactly what to do and how to do it.

"Therefore, leaving the elementary teachings about the Christ..." Does that mean we abandon the teachings of Christ? Of course not. We do not abandon the laying on of hands, we do not abandon teaching about the resurrection and judgment, or any other of the basics. But the reason the body of Christ has remained in infancy is that we have refused to walk in love and to grow up. We have spent a lot of time throwing rocks at each other because we have been so insecure in our places. We have had to tear somebody else down to elevate ourselves. It is just like a bunch of children fussing and fighting. That is what kids do! It is time to grow up!

Theology of Martyrdom

We have to begin to see the larger purposes of the Kingdom of God. We have expected God to scoop us off the earth to protect us, but this has not happened. There have been more people martyred for Christ in the last forty years than throughout all of recorded history! We have recently found out about the atrocities in China and the Soviet Union that have seen millions upon millions of Christians slaughtered. Some of us may be martyrs, but no one should fear martyrdom.

Let us consider martyrdom from the point of view of the Scriptures. First, we should be encouraged by the passage "...God is faithful, who will not allow you to be tempted beyond what you are able, but with the temptation will provide the way of escape also, that you may be able to endure it" (1 Cor. 10:13). Many of us would say, "I could never handle martyrdom." If God can make a way of escape from temptation, then if we could not handle martyrdom He would not allow us to go that route. He would spare us. But there will be people who will be martyred!

In the seventh chapter of the Book of Acts we find one of the most beautiful pictures of martyrdom in the Word of God. This is Stephen's death. He has already preached his message to the religious people of his day; then in verses 54-60 we read this account: "Now when they heard this, they were cut to the quick, and they began gnashing their teeth at him. But being full of the Holy Spirit, he gazed intently into heaven and saw the glory of God, and Jesus standing at the right hand of God; and he said, 'Behold, I see the heavens opened up and the Son of Man standing at the right hand of God.' But they cried out with a loud voice, and covered their ears, and they rushed upon him with one impulse. And when they had driven him out of the city, they began stoning him, and the witnesses laid aside their robes at the feet of a young man named Saul. And they went on stoning Stephen as he called upon the Lord and said, 'Lord Jesus, receive my spirit!' And falling on his knees, he cried out with a loud voice, 'Lord, do not hold this sin against them!' And having said this..." [What happens next? He died a horrible, painful, bloody, agonizing death? NO! What really happened?] He fell asleep"! Each one of us does that at least once a day. Big deal. He fell asleep.

Consider how most people die today. They wind up in intensive care units of hospitals, hooked up to tubes and machines. It is appointed unto every man to die. So which way would most of us choose? We could wind up in intensive care with all those tubes, or be "rocked" to sleep like Stephen. Our problem is that we have such tunnel vision. We just see tiny little pieces of God's plan. God is after believers who can come to a place of real maturity where they can be pillars in the house of God. He is looking for those who have a word in due season for people who are hurting. He wants people who can discern needs in the community. His desire is that our evangelistic fervor would grow more intense day by day because of our covenant relationship with the Lord.

The Place of Persecution

God is in control. He has not appointed us unto wrath, but unto salvation. Those whom the Lord loves, He does chasten. No one has ever died from the Lord's chastening. God does not beat us to death. He just gets our attention. Sometimes He has to use rather drastic measures. It is called "tough love"!

"For the sake of My name I delay my wrath" (Is. 48:9). Let us consider that word "wrath." The wrath of

God has been building up for 6,000 years. The Bible tells us that when God's wrath has really reached the full, that's when the end of the age comes — when He is fed up with those who have totally rejected His plan of salvation. First Thessalonians 5:9 says, "For God has not destined us for wrath, but for obtaining salvation through our Lord Jesus Christ." So who gets God's wrath? It is those who mess with us!

There is a big difference between persecution and tribulation. All who live godly in Christ Jesus shall suffer persecution. We live in a very sheltered society in America. If someone looks at us wrong, we call that persecution. In other countries they know what persecution is. Consider the story of a little Russian girl. The KGB caught her as she was going to a prayer meeting. She had her Bible hidden under her coat. She was terrified when they stopped her. They asked where she was going and she started to cry. She said, "I'm going to a family gathering." They asked her, "What are you going to do when you get there?" She responded, "We are going to read my father's will." They felt sorry for her and let her go! That is God's hand of deliverance!

God does give immunity. God does give protection. The people who are going to be in trouble are the ones who are hanging around on the outskirts of the camp, people who are not totally committed to God. There are a lot of people who have some head knowledge, who want to play games with God. They want to attend church a few Sundays out of the year and dabble out there in the world. They are going to be in serious trouble! They will be the first ones picked off when problems come. The immunity of the believer is really in knowing Jesus. When we are walking in obedience to the Lord, a thousand will fall at our left hand, and ten thousand at our right hand, but it shall not come near us!

Let's look again at Isaiah 48. "For the sake of My name I delay my wrath, and for My praise I restrain it for you, in order not to cut you off. Behold, I have refined you, but not as silver; I have tested you in the furnace of affliction. For My own sake, for My own sake, I will act; for how can My name be profaned? And My glory I will not give to another" (vv. 9-11). The Lord is running a tight ship. He wants us to be squeaky clean. It is not a matter of legalism. It is a matter of going on in God. Through the Holy Spirit we are being taught and led in Christ. It is almost indescribable what God has presented to this generation. The prophets who lived in ages past looked to this day and wished they could be a part of it. We will be the ones who will help culminate the age by our own obedience to the Word.

Paul's Words of Encouragement

Let us examine the words of Paul, Silvanus, and Timothy. In chapter one verses 3-12 of Second Thessalonians we read: "We ought always to give thanks to God for you, brethren, as it is only fitting, because your faith is greatly enlarged, and the love of each one of you toward one another grows ever greater; therefore, we ourselves speak proudly of you among the churches of God for your perseverance and faith in the midst of all your persecutions and afflictions which you endure. This is a plain indication of God's righteous judgment so that you may be considered worthy of the kingdom of God, for which indeed you are suffering. [Notice this does not say that we are going to be considered worthy to go to heaven. It says we are going to be considered worthy of our inheritance, to obtain the Kingdom of God and to walk in it.] For after all it is only just for God to repay with affliction those who afflict you, and to give relief to you who are afflicted and to us as well when the Lord Jesus shall be revealed from heaven with His mighty angels in flaming fire, dealing out retribution to those who do not know God and to those who do not obey the gospel of our Lord Jesus. [Once again we see different categories of people; those who do not know God and those who do not obey the gospel]. And these will pay the penalty of eternal destruction, away from the presence of the Lord [The penalty of disobedience is to be away from the presence of the Lord. That is the beginning of hell!] and from the glory of His power, when He comes to be glorified in His saints on that day, and to be marveled at among all who have believed — for our testimony to you was believed. To this end also we pray for you always that our God may count you worthy of your calling, and fulfill every desire for goodness and the work of faith with power; in order that the name of our Lord Jesus may be glorified in you, and you in Him [He is not only going to be glorified in us, but we are going to be glorified in Him. That is why He is after righteousness, because He wants to say, "You are glorified in Me." It is a two-way street! And so it shall be.], according to the grace of our God and the Lord Jesus Christ." Amen.

Isaiah wrote, "But now, thus says the Lord, your Creator, O Jacob, and He who formed you, O Israel, 'Do not fear, for I have redeemed you; I have called you by name; you are Mine! When you pass through the waters, I will be with you; and through the rivers, though they will not overflow you. When you walk through the fire, you will not be scorched, nor will the flame burn you. For I am the Lord your God..." (Is. 43:1-3).

CHAPTER SIX

What About Our Mansions?

Building a House for God

In Second Chronicles chapter two, we read these words: "Now Solomon decided to build a house for the name of the Lord, and a royal palace for himself ...Behold, I am about to build a house for the name of the Lord my God, dedicating it to Him...And the house which I am about to build will be great; for greater is our God than all the gods" (vv. 1, 4-5). As we approach the next verse, we see Solomon's concern about the temple that he is about to build. For he says in verse 6, "But who is able to build a house for Him, for the heavens and the highest heavens cannot contain Him? So who am I, that I should build a house for Him, except to burn incense before Him?" Seven times in this second chapter, Solomon refers to the temple as the "house" of God. The third chapter of Second Chronicles gives the details of the construction of the temple, which again is referred to as the "house" of God (seven more times). The fourth chapter chronicles the furnishings of the temple and refers to it as the "house" of God six times. Chapter five records the completion of the temple, mentioning it as the "house" of God four more times. The highlight of this chapter is when the priests come forth from the holy place, along with all the Levitical singers. We see one hundred and twenty priests blowing trumpets in unison; joining them were the singers, who with one voice praised the Lord saying, "He indeed is good for His lovingkindness is everlasting" (v. 13). The Scripture goes on to say that the "house" of the Lord was filled with a cloud, so that the priests could not stand to minister, for the glory of the Lord filled the house of God.

From the second chapter of Second Chronicles through verse one of chapter eight, the temple is referred to fifty-one times as the "house" of God. In the sixth chapter of Second Chronicles, verse 18, Solomon expresses his concern about the temple being adequate for God to dwell in: "But will God indeed dwell with mankind on the earth? Behold, heaven and the highest heaven cannot contain Thee; how much less this house which I have built." This glorious temple that Solomon built was to be so profaned by the hypocrisy of the Jews that when Jesus walked into it and saw the activity that was going on, He said to the money changers, "It is written, 'My house shall be called a house of prayer'; but you are making it a robbers' den."

Seven hundred and fourteen years earlier, God had already checked out of the temple, and we find His attitude about it in Isaiah 66:1-2: "Thus says the Lord, 'Heaven is My throne, and the earth is My footstool. Where then is a house you could build for Me? And where is a place that I may rest? For My hand made all these things, thus all these things came into being...' "

In the next phrase we see something astounding.

God tells us where He is going to dwell. He goes on to say, "But TO THIS ONE I will look, To HIM who is humble and contrite of spirit, and who trembles at My word."

God was so grieved with the Jews' religious hypocrisy that He scorns their burnt offerings. In Isaiah 66:3-4 the Lord says, "But he who kills an ox is like one who slays a man; he who sacrifices a lamb is like the one who breaks a dog's neck; he who offers a grain offering is like one who offers swine's blood; he who burns incense is like the one who blesses an idol. As they have chosen their own ways, and their soul delights in their abominations, so I will choose their punishments, and I will bring on them what they dread. Because I called, but no one answered; I spoke, but they did not listen. And they did evil in My sight, and chose that in which I did not delight."

So where is God going to dwell? In a humble and contrite spirit. God checked out of buildings! According to First Corinthians 3:16, YOU are His temple if you are a believer. Paul says it this way: "Do you not know that you are a temple of God, and the Spirit of God dwells in you?" When the revelation of God's Kingdom begins to dawn and we see that God's intent is for the meek to inherit the earth, the question always arises, "What about our mansions?"

The problem is that there never were any to begin with. We have taken a word out of the *King James Version* and built a doctrine around it. For that translation says, in John 14:2-3, "In My Father's house are many mansions: if it were not so, I would have told you. I go to prepare a place for you. And if I go and prepare a place for you, I will come again, and receive you unto myself; that where I am, there ye may be also." The word "mansion," as we know it, is not in the original Greek text. It is the King James English equivalent of "house" or "abode," a poor house of the common people — not a king's castle. Most translators have corrected that passage to read: "In My Father's house are many DWELLING PLACES." If God checked out of the temple in Isaiah 66 and if Jesus went into the temple with a whip and rebuked the people for their profane activity, and if Paul says, "Do you not know that YOU are a temple of God," then we need to know what this new temple really is.

Let's turn to the Scriptures and build this new temple block by block. Psalm 118:22 gives us our first clue as to the material used in the construction of this new temple. "The stone which the builders rejected has become the chief corner stone." Jesus Himself is the main building block in this new temple, which is also referred to in Daniel 2:34. Here Daniel is interpreting King Nebuchadnezzar's dream concerning the future. In verses 34 and 35, he told Nebuchadnezzar, "You continued looking until a stone was cut out without hands, and it struck the statue on its feet of iron and clay, and crushed them. Then the iron, the clay, the bronze, the silver and the gold were crushed all at the same time, and became like chaff from the summer threshing floors; and the wind carried them away so that not a trace of them was found. But the stone that struck the statue became a great mountain and filled the whole earth." Daniel goes on to say in verses 44 and 45, "And in the days of those kings the God of heaven will set up a kingdom which will never be destroyed, and that kingdom will not be left for another people; it will crush and put an end to all these kingdoms, but it will itself endure forever. Inasmuch as you saw that a stone was cut out of the mountain without hands and that it crushed the iron, the bronze, the clay, the silver, and the gold, the great God has made known to the king what will take place in the future; so the dream is true, and its interpretation is trustworthy.''

So we see in Psalm 118:22 and in Daniel 2:34 that Jesus is the Stone that the builders rejected and the Stone that was cut out of the mountain which filled the whole earth, which is a picture of the Church and the Kingdom. It's a picture of the Church because Jesus is the chief corner Stone (Eph. 2:20). It's a type of the Kingdom because He is that Stone that struck the statue, which represents every form of human government; that stone, according to Daniel 2:35, became a great mountain (or Kingdom) which filled the whole earth.

Let's follow this train of thought into the New Testament. In Matthew 21:33-44 Jesus teaches using this parable: "Listen to another parable. There was a landowner who planted a vineyard and put a wall around it and dug a wine press in it, and built a tower, and rented it out to vine-growers, and went on a journey. And when the harvest time approached, he sent his slaves to the vine-growers to receive his produce. And the vine-growers took his slaves and beat one, and killed another, and stoned a third. Again he sent another group of slaves larger than the first; and they did the same thing to them. But afterward he sent his son to them, saying, 'They will respect my son.' But when the vine-growers saw the son, they said among themselves, 'This is the heir; come, let us kill him, and seize his inheritance.' And they took him, and threw him out of the vineyard, and killed him. Therefore when the owner of the vineyard comes, what will he do to those vine-growers?'' Little did they know that they were the very vine-growers Jesus was talking about. Verse 41 continues, "They said to Him, 'He will bring those wretches to a wretched end, and will rent out the vineyard to other vine-growers, who will pay him the proceeds at the proper seasons.' Jesus said to them, 'Did you never read in the Scriptures, "The stone which the builders rejected, this became the chief corner stone; this came about from the Lord, and it is marvelous in our eyes"? Therefore I say to you, the kingdom of God will be taken away from you, and be given to a nation producing the fruit of it. And he who falls on this stone will be broken to pieces; but on whomever it falls, it will scatter him like dust.' "

God checked out of their temple in Isaiah 66 because they had already become apostate. This parable teaches that, because of their rejection of Jesus as King, the Kingdom is stripped from them and is given to a nation producing the fruit of it. Who is that nation? It's a people who were not a people — the Gentiles. We are still looking for that new temple of which Jesus is the chief corner Stone. First Peter 2:4-10 gives us more insight: "And coming to Him, as to a *living stone*, rejected by men, but choice and precious in the sight of God, YOU ALSO, AS LIVING STONES, are being built up as a *SPIRITUAL HOUSE* for a holy priesthood, to offer up spiritual sacrifices acceptable to God through Jesus Christ. For this is contained in Scripture: 'Behold I lay in Zion a choice stone, a precious corner stone, and he who believes in Him shall not be disappointed.' This precious value, then, is for you who believe. But for those who disbelieve, 'The stone which the builders rejected, this became the very corner stone,' and, 'a stone of stumbling and a rock of offense'; for they stumble because they are disobedient to the word, and to this doom they were also appointed. But you are a chosen race, a royal priesthood, a holy nation, a people for God's own possession, that you may proclaim the excellencies of Him who has called you out of darkness into His marvelous light; for you once were not a people, but now you are the people of God; you had not received mercy, but now you have received mercy."

This new temple, according to Peter, is made up of *living* stones. From these living stones, the Lord is building a *spiritual house*. Jesus gave a scathing denunciation of the self-righteousness of the scribes and Pharisees in Matthew 23. After repeatedly calling them hypocrites, fools, blind guides, and serpents, He concluded with these words: "O Jerusalem, Jerusalem, who kills the prophets and stones those who are sent to her! How often I wanted to gather your children together, the way a hen gathers her chicks under her wings, and you were unwilling. Behold, your house is being left to you desolate!" (Matt. 23:37-38) Remember, all through the Scriptures, "temple" is synonymous with "house." When Jesus said, "Behold your house is being left to you desolate," He is telling them that their temple is going to be left desolate. When Jesus walked out of the temple at the end of this declaration, He would never reenter it. Verses one and two of Chapter 24 conclude this phase of Christ's ministry, for we read: "And Jesus came out from the temple and was going away when His disciples came up to point out the temple buildings to Him. And He answered and said to them, 'Do you not see all these things? Truly I say to you, not one stone here shall be left upon another, which will not be torn down.' " When the disciples followed Jesus out of the temple, they were in shock. They had never seen Jesus so angry. In an attempt to get Him in a good mood, they began to point out the beauty of the temple, forgetting that Jesus had just said that it was going to be left desolate. What they had held in such high esteem, Jesus had condemned. His prophecy was fulfilled when Titus went through Jerusalem in 70 A.D. with his army and literally tore the temple apart stone by stone.

We have seen that the words "house" and "temple" are interchangeable in meaning and usage. With this in mind, let us turn to John 14 and examine the traditional text referring to mansions. Verse 2 says, "In My Father's *house* are many DWELLING PLACES..." (NAS; this is the correct translation from the original Greek). The inference is that His *NEW HOUSE* would be comprised of humble and contrite spirits. He went on to say "...for I go to prepare a place [not "mansion") for you." What is that place? It's a place of authority! Has He not given us the keys to the Kingdom? Has He not given us power over the enemy? Wherever you are geographically at this moment, if you are a true believer, are you not also seated together with Christ in *heavenly places* (Eph. 2:4-6)?

We have seen in First Peter chapter two that we are referred to as living stones, and that we are a spiritual house. What about our mansions? There never were any to begin with. Religious people have been building sandcastles for years out of a mistranslated word. From now on, when you read that text in John 14:2, you should read it, "In My Father's house are many dwelling places." And every time you look at a believer, the thought should go through your mind, "There's one; there's another one." To cap this revelation off, let's look at Hebrews 3:1-6: "Therefore, holy brethren, partakers of a heavenly calling, consider Jesus, the Apostle and High Priest of our confession. He was faithful to Him who appointed Him, as Moses also was in all His house. For He has been counted worthy of more glory than Moses, by just so much as the builder of the house has more honor than the house. For every house is built by someone, but the builder of all things is God. Now Moses was faithful in all His house as a servant, for a testimony of those things which were to be spoken later; but Christ was faithful as a Son over *His house whose house we are*, if we hold fast our confidence and the boast of our hope firm until the end." We are the temple of the living God! Christ in us is our hope of glory, and He is coming forth in a many-membered body. He is coming forth to be glorified in His saints.

Books are available from:

**Mel Bailey Ministries
P.O. Box 895
Mukilteo, WA 98275**